Praise for *Buddhis*

'Buddhist practitioner Napthali has written an eminently practical book that gives frazzled mothers useable advice and empathy . . . precisely because she is not a teacher and is in the midst of mothering, Napthali offers the approachable and authentic perspective of a rank-and-file practitioner who lives the techniques and situations she writes about.'—*Publishers Weekly*

'Napthali's book focuses on Buddhist practices that will help mothers become calmer and happier in themselves. Follow her advice and we all know what comes next—better parenting.'—*Sunday Telegraph*

'Funny, uplifting, reassuring, real and wise. A truly "mothering" book for mothers . . .'—Stephanie Dowrick

'This is an excellent, practical guide to everyday Buddhism, not just for mothers, but for everyone who has ever had a mother.'—Vicki Mackenzie, author of the best-selling *Why Buddhism?*

'Buddhism for Mothers is an oasis of calm and tranquility in the otherwise chaotic existence that is motherhood.'—*Mind & Body*

'This is Buddhism at its most accessible.'—*Conscious Living*

'. . . approach the day-to-day "highs and lows" differently and more positively, and yes—even more calmly.'—Childbirth Education Association

Reviews from Amazon

'I love this book. It brings such a calming sense of being just by picking it up.'—Kathleen

'I love this book! I would recommend this book to anyone, Buddhist or not. I'm so glad someone is finally talking about how to deal with the stresses of mother hood in a realistic way without inducing guilt or fear. The author's tone is both friendly and empathetic—just what we moms need. The book is empowering and has made a big difference in the way I parent and the way I view my life as a mom.'—T. M.-R.

'The author is very honest and refreshing. On every page you get the sense that the author is a very real person who can relate to both the best and the stressed in us all.'—Suzanne

'IF YOU'RE A MOM, BUY THIS BOOK! I am sceptical of anyone trying to preach an idea to me, and I do not claim to be Buddhist. I just LOVE this book. I checked it out from a local library, but am now purchasing it so I can always have it around. It not only approaches ways to be a calmer mom, but a calmer being in your daily encounter with the world. It has changed how I approach issues, big or small; it's also inspired me to demonstrate the same zen-buddhist coping tools for my children; and it has helped me to stay in the present moment.'—Kristin

Praise for *Buddhism for Mothers with Young Children* (formerly titled *Buddhism for Mothers with Lingering Questions*)

'Napthali is a lovely writer. She skilfully weaves interviews with other parents into her own thoughts. As for guilt, Tibetans don't even have a word for it, she writes.'—*Sydney Morning Herald*

'If you liked her first book, *Buddhism for Mothers*, then you'll adore this one. It'll give you a new perspective on parenting and may even help you enjoy it more.'—*Sunday Telegraph*

'This second book from Sarah Napthali . . . had me repeatedly crying out "yes" . . . By being focused, open and more attentive to the present moment we can enjoy a calmer and happier journey through parenthood; a great companion book for mothers struggling to cope with their new role.'—*Perth Woman*

'There is much here to learn; through Napthali's eyes, patience, reflection and calm become the vehicles to a deeper understanding of self, motherhood and family.'—*Junior*

SARAH NAPTHALI

Buddhism
for MOTHERS of
SCHOOLCHILDREN

FINDING CALM IN THE
CHAOS OF THE SCHOOL YEARS

inspired
LIVING

ALLEN&UNWIN

Other books by Sarah Napthali

Buddhism for Mothers

Buddhism for Mothers of Young Children
(previously published as *Buddhism for Mothers
with Lingering Questions*)

First published in 2009

Inspired Living, an imprint of
Allen & Unwin
83 Alexander Street
Crows Nest NSW 2065
Australia
Phone: (61 2) 8425 0100
Fax: (61 2) 9906 2218
Email: info@allenandunwin.com
Web: www.allenandunwin.com

Cataloguing-in-Publication details are available
from the National Library of Australia
www.librariesaustralia.nla.gov.au

ISBN 978 1 74175 697 5

Set in 11/15 pt Adobe Garamond Pro by Bookhouse, Sydney
Printed and bound in Australia by Griffin Press

10 9 8 7 6 5 4 3 2 1

The poem on pages 94–5 is reprinted from *Call Me By My True Names*
(1999) by Thich Nhat Hanh with permission of Parallax Press, Berkeley,
California, www.parallax.org.

contents

preface

FEW SIGHTS ARE AS TOUCHING or as emotionally overwhelming as that of our child releasing our hand and walking off to the classroom on the first day of school. The pre-school years are over. Our responsibilities shift and we find ourselves beginners once more. Raising schoolchildren proves to be a radically different experience from tending our under-fives. Amateurs once again, we face a new stage of motherhood each time one of our children starts school.

These early school years are, for many of us, the golden years of parenting, the hard-earned window between demanding toddlerhood and unpredictable adolescence. Yet challenges still abound. Our children have varying capacities to adapt to the school system and their ability to fit in dictates the state of our mental health. Unlike the toddler years, we can at least reason with a school-aged child to a far greater extent, but in most cases teaching them to take responsibility for themselves calls for bottomless depths of patience.

The day our youngest starts school is one we may have fantasised about for years, yet many mothers find themselves grieving the end of a stage in parenthood. Sales of tissues mushroom as mothers everywhere pat the tears they try to hide from their children. For many of us this milestone signifies a return to the workforce, an increase in working hours or a sudden pressure to decide what to do with the rest of our lives. Whether we feel like a traumatised empty-nester or a woman who finally has her life back, our sense of identity shifts: we do not feel like the same person we were a year ago. Our role has changed, as has our relationship with time: there are more hours in our week, or, if we increase our work hours, even less.

Personally, I shed not a tear when Alex, my younger son, started school, and I have never looked back for even a minute. Although my love for Alex and the delight I often feel in his company is beyond measure, I had played enough hours of hide-and-seek, had co-baked a sufficient number of cakes and had left no corner of the zoo unexplored. Maybe I was influenced by my experience with Alex's older brother Zac, but I harboured a preference for the company of school-aged children over the under-five set: Zac had been a challenging youngster but after starting school had blossomed into the most pleasant boy, notwithstanding occasional lapses. Zac had been so enthusiastic about his first year of school that I could not help but look forward to a similar experience for Alex. I was definitely ready.

The mother load eased significantly, yet new sources of stress arose. For school mothers, the deadlines in our lives multiply: school by nine, pick up by three, homework done by seven, bedtime by a reasonable hour, and we must arrive on time for sporting commitments and a host of other after-school activities. Fortunately, the teachings of the Buddha are highly relevant for managing stress, a topic I tackle in the first two chapters. Some Buddhist teachers even prefer to translate the Buddha's First Noble Truth, 'There is suffering', as, 'There is stress', arguing the latter captures a wider range of unsatisfactory experiences.

One of our greatest challenges as mothers of schoolchildren is managing time: fitting umpteen tasks into a limited period, living as potential slaves to our 'to do' list, and the gnawing sense of failure around how effectively we use our day. With children at school we might have looked forward to several additional hours in our week only to be amazed at how quickly they are swallowed up by new responsibilities. Our children may be at school yet we still careen through our day, never accomplishing all our goals.

Now more than ever, we find ourselves living a routine. We prepare children for school, we collect them of an afternoon and spend many hours on the responsibilities of the evening, which can start to feel the same, day after day. Some mothers complain of a sense of reliving the same day without end. While the security of a routine can feel comforting, at times it bores us witless and we grapple with restlessness and discontent. As we shall find in Chapter 3, Buddhist teachings offer fresh perspectives for perceiving our surroundings, and help us to look at some of the causes behind boredom and how we can eliminate them.

Other challenges we find ourselves fielding are the tricky questions our children hurl at us, sometimes at moments less than ideal for such discussions. Schoolchildren require answers about sex, death, God, government and human cruelty. Many of us need to revisit, rethink or at least clarify our viewpoints before we can present them for the perspective of a child. As modern parents discussing the heavy issues, we avoid seeing our children as empty vessels waiting to have all our views and opinions poured into them, and heed the Buddha's warnings against being attached to any of our views. A Buddhist approach, as presented in Chapter 4, allows us to share our values with our children while still empowering them to think for themselves and reach their own conclusions.

Significantly, with children at school, we belong to a new community. Unable to select the members of this collective, we are obliged to blend in as best we can. How we yearn, as human beings with our herd instinct, for a sense of belonging. While some of us are able to fulfil this need within the parent community, others among us, for all kinds of reasons, never will—or will need months, years even, to identify potential friends. All these new families in our lives may provide us with the priceless gifts of friendship, support and happy memories. Yet some of these relationships challenge us, presenting moral dilemmas as well as the need to compromise or establish boundaries. Chapter 5 provides some Buddhist perspectives on this fraught area.

Just as in the toddler years, feelings of guilt continue to haunt many mothers of schoolchildren. Am I a good enough mother? Do I give my children enough of my time? Am I missing some of their most important moments? Do I yell too much? Am I as good as my own mother was? Am I letting my children down in any way? Am I pleasing everybody? Doing everything well enough? All these questions are worth asking, ideally with a non-judgemental, inquiring attitude. Yet if they gnaw away at us, undermining our happiness on a daily basis without our ever resolving them, then we might need to look more deeply at what is going on. Several chapters will address this topic pervading the lives of most mothers.

One mother in particular, Camilla, will feature in this book. Camilla has two boys and a girl, aged twelve, ten and eight respectively. Camilla is passionate about the Buddha's teachings and loves nothing more than to retire to a quiet corner for a deep conversation about their potential. She speaks slowly and deliberately, punctuating many sentences with the words 'for *me*', as if to emphasise that she has learned what works for herself but never assumes she has an answer for the rest of humanity.

Yet what impressed me most about her practice was the number of success stories. Through practising what the Buddha taught she has managed to give up quite a string of behaviours that undermined her potential to be happy—smoking, gossiping and moping about past mistakes, to name a few. I had been dying to ask her if I could interview her for my last book but I was too shy. I could not bear the idea of her refusing and the ensuing awkwardness of seeing her every week at my Buddhist group. Finally, for this book I found the courage to ask her, albeit via email. And yes, she was initially reluctant, but fortunately she changed her mind, after talking to her mother.

I met Camilla at my Buddhist group, where she was the secretary of the committee. I found, whenever I spoke to her, she would say something that inspired me for days afterwards. In one of our conversations I was bewailing how much housework mothers need to do and she stumped me with, 'Oh, I love housework—I just practise mindfulness.' She wasn't trying to make me feel inferior—she meant it. On another occasion Camilla told me, 'I grew up in a wealthy household that was very unhappy so I have no need to chase money: I know from first-hand experience that it doesn't make you happy.'

With a passion for philosophy and science, Camilla has begun to feel distinctly lukewarm about the prospect of continuing her profession of accountancy, especially given the number of hours it devours from her week. Camilla works four days a week and the children catch a bus after school to her work, from where she drives them home. On the home front, she has managed the small miracle of a happy, inspiring marriage, capable as she is of praising her husband, a carpenter, frequently and at length.

Having attended some Buddhist events with Camilla outside Sydney, I found opportunities for long conversations and I have come to know her rather well. I know, for example, that she would be mortified to think I might portray her as some kind of Buddhist model for mothers and she would be at pains to convince everyone that she is a very ordinary mother with a great deal of spiritual work still ahead of her. If the truth be known, she has no faith whatsoever in the possibility of ever becoming fully enlightened. She just sees herself as benefitting from the journey towards that goal.

Camilla, like most mothers, has embarked on an exciting period of personal growth. As mothers of school-aged children we see ourselves going beyond what we ever thought we were capable of. We witness in ourselves extremes of anger that shock us, as much as we see more love in our hearts than we ever imagined could exist. Learning more about what we are capable of, and owning all of it, is the point from which we grow spiritually. Walking a spiritual path, we start to notice the potential for our self-confidence to come not from any limited concept of a self with its set strengths and weaknesses, but from a faith in our growing connection with our inner wisdom.

As with my past books, I have taken the unconventional approach of drawing on Buddhist teachings from all the main traditions: Zen, Tibetan and Theravada (the latter being practised in Sri Lanka and most of the countries of South-East Asia). Yet in practice, committed Buddhists choose a teacher, or several, from one of the main schools and settle there. This prevents them from endlessly skirting about the surface of Buddhism and allows them to go more deeply into their chosen practice. They see a risk in treating Buddhism like a spiritual supermarket for too long, where we follow all our whims and impulses, attracted to novelties and fleeing challenges.

One reason I draw from all the main schools is in order to help mothers decide which school most attracts them. Another reason is that almost all the books we find about Buddhism present the perspective of one tradition, so it is interesting to present the different perspectives in one place. That said, the core teachings of Buddhism are the same in every tradition. The differences lie more in *how* to practise: the meditation techniques, the subtly different priorities, and the varying reliance on ritual.

Drawing from the experiences of my own family as I wrote this book, I did ask permission from my sons to share any potentially embarrassing stories and they have been generous with their permission. Zac was initially hesitant about one or two stories, but these feelings were nothing a new yo-yo couldn't fix. My husband Marek has always given me carte blanche to disclose whatever I wish about him. He does not mind what I write possibly because he does not—*cannot*—read my books, declaring matters spiritual 'not his thing'. Although I secretly pine for him to join me on the road to enlightenment, he is an engineer, I am a writer, and it is part of my spiritual practice to respect our differences without forcing him to recreate himself in my image.

I have not written a book telling mothers how to parent for I am sure that they know better than me what works in their unique situation—and books abound by authors more knowledgeable than myself about child-rearing. Most of the chapters in this book focus on the needs of the mother, recognising that when we are in good form we can only be wiser and more skilful mothers, and this benefits our children. How, as mothers of schoolchildren, can we bring our best selves to the task of mothering so that we are not at the mercy of daily frustrations, fears and anxieties? How can we rise above habitual reactions of irritability, stress and impatience? And what are the most reliable sources of contentment for us? These are the questions this book grapples with, by exploring teachings tested over two and a half millennia.

CHAPTER 1

stress

MOTHERS OF SCHOOLCHILDREN CAN have a tense relationship with time and, in some cases, an obsessive attachment to using it efficiently. One of the greatest injuries one can commit against a mother is to waste her time. Any form of time-wasting feels painful and sees our stress levels soar: traffic, red lights, queues, a stalled computer, even a minute of idle conversation. It is worth being aware of our relationship with time, especially of the costs of being overly attached to using it efficiently. Does our relationship with time mean, for example, we have less time for connection with our children, family and friends? Does it affect our whole capacity to relax and be content, even when on holiday? How does it affect our general mood and attitude to others? Do we create more pressure on ourselves than there needs to be?

The Buddha did not sit down to meditate under the Bodhi tree intending to devise a list of stress-management techniques. He was far more ambitious than that for he was on a quest for nothing less than liberation from suffering. That said, mothers can lead quite stressful lives and practising Buddhist teachings offers a way to attack the stress at its various sources. To lead less stressful lives we need to create conditions of balance in our lifestyle, refusing to become perpetually driven, refusing to sacrifice our lives to the culture of busyness. We explore the topics of balance and the avoidance of extremes in the next chapter, but there are many other offerings from Buddhist teachings to help us reduce stress and this chapter presents a smorgasbord for you to choose from.

The first step in dealing with stress is in acknowledging that, despite all appearances, it comes not from 'out there' but from inside us, in our response. While we can work on changing or controlling our external conditions to some degree, the way to bring about a lasting reduction in stress is by working on how we habitually respond to the events of our lives. We can always put a temporary bandaid over a stress breakout—drink some alcohol, watch telly, pretend it's not happening—or maybe we can look more deeply as a means to dropping our less helpful reactions.

BE WITH THE STRESS

One aspect I have noticed about my own experience of stress is aversion, a rejection of the stress I feel. I notice the presence of stress and instantly panic: *no, you can't be stressed, you must be calm, you must appear cool and laid-back*. I might then try to suppress or deny the stress. Or I am harsh on myself: I feel guilty for being stressed, or even angry at myself. Clearly, such a reaction to noticing stress only compounds it.

Yet a simple Buddhist approach is perfectly available to me. I can pause and slowly say, 'Stress is here now,' and leave it right there. I do not need to reject, suppress, deny, ignore or distract. I can simply *be with* the stress.

The Buddhist approach deals similarly with anger, sadness or restlessness. We can simply say, 'Anger is here now,' or 'Sadness is here now,' or 'Restlessness is here now,' and then be with it. This quality of *being* requires of us not only compassion but also curiosity. What is anger actually like? What is sadness, restlessness or stress actually like? How do they feel in my body? What does it feel like in my mind? How long does it last? Does it change in intensity? The answer to the last question, in every case, is *Yes*—of this we can be sure. None of these mind states are permanent, no matter how intense they feel at the time. They are only transitory mind phenomena which we do not need to believe or trust.

Importantly, we can be with our feelings of stress compassionately— that is, with some compassion towards ourselves—rather than adding our usual harsh judgements that try to dictate whether or not we should feel the way we do.

I once met a self-described 'stress prone' mother who told me that when she meditated she would sometimes say to herself, 'Settle, Petal.' While my first reaction was to laugh at her corniness, on reflection I understood the gentleness in her words, so motherly and nurturing. Such a level of compassion for self is worth cultivating, both during meditation and throughout times of stress. I apologised to the mother for laughing.

We try to cultivate curiosity towards our feelings of stress, asking ourselves, 'What is going on here?' Of course, when we are extremely stressed, we find that we don't particularly *care* what is going on. We might feel so frustrated that we have no energy left to turn inward. Still, we can always reflect back later and ask, 'What *was* going on then?' Senior Buddhist teacher Christopher Titmuss even goes so far as to say that curiosity is the most important quality of all to bring to Buddhist practice.

Not adding stuff

For many years, Camilla found the morning routine of preparing three children for school extremely stressful. She started paying closer attention to her mind throughout this process and discovered fear and many thoughts:

If we are late then:

- I'll feel like an incompetent mother.
- I'll be seen by parents and teachers as a hopeless case.
- I will let down three teachers and three classes full of children.
- I will feel cranky about failing to achieve a simple task that millions of mothers around the world perform daily.

These thoughts also arose for her:

- My children don't even care if they are late. I am the only responsible person here.
- My children are purposely trying to provoke me.
- If we're late once it will happen every day.
- This rushing and battling happens every single day!

Camilla was able to ease up about the whole morning routine when she saw clearly how much drama she was adding. Laughing, she wonders why she ever expected her children to care about being late: 'They're kids! Do I really want them to behave like up-tight adults?' As a regular meditator committed to mindfulness—the practice of purposely 'remembering' the present—Camilla is impressively capable of seeing both what is happening as well as the possibility of letting go of any thoughts that lead to suffering and stress. Mornings are still hard work as she teaches her children to take more responsibility for the process, but these days she is no longer so stressed about them.

An invaluable question we can ask ourselves when we feel stressed is, 'What am I adding?' Everything we go through in life is made up of a pure experience plus all the things we tell ourselves about the experience. Buddhists strive to perceive the pure experience, free from biases, drama, clinging and our need for a positive self-image.

In *A Path for Parents*, mother of two schoolchildren Sara Burns describes how she brings Buddhist teachings to daily motherhood. In this case, to preparing dinner:

The Buddha suggested that two 'arrows' hit us every time something happens to us. The first is the event itself, the second is how we react to it . . . One example for me would be walking into the kitchen to cook, feeling tired and wishing someone else was there to produce a delicious meal and look after me . . . But on top of this I could unconsciously pile secondary arrows, along the lines of, 'It's always the same,' 'This is never-ending,' 'I'll never have enough sleep,' 'No one cares for me,' 'I can't cope.' These arrows pile on the pain making the situation much worse and taking me even further from my simple desire that my children and I are well fed and happy, from confidence that I can do what is necessary, and from the possibility of a more creative response, such as cooking what I like for once instead of what my children like.

So next time we feel overwhelmed, consider the arrows. What is the first arrow? The event itself? And what are the subsequent arrows, or the thoughts we are adding that only inflate the stress? You will probably also see your beliefs of what *ought* to be happening and, if you are spiritually switched on, the possibility of clinging to these beliefs a little more loosely or letting go altogether.

With our tendency to think too much—to analyse, deconstruct, reconstruct and ruminate—we deny ourselves the simplicity of pure experiences. We conduct post-mortems on past conversations, study the deeper meaning of a remark someone made in passing, evaluate our performance at the parent meeting or compulsively plan the future rather than enjoy our day. Why not live more of our lives with an openness to the present moment, instead of being mired in our heads, entangled in thoughts that only 'add' to what actually happens?

REACTING TO DIFFICULTIES

As I mentioned in opening this book, the Buddha taught in his First Noble Truth that there is suffering, stress and unsatisfactoriness, that is, *dukkha*. So it follows that life can be difficult. Parenting, in particular, is by its very nature difficult. Interestingly, once we accept and deeply understand that life can be difficult, then life, and parenting too, become significantly less difficult. By railing against the difficulty and allowing it to make us angry or anxious every time it arises, we are being unrealistic and multiplying our capacity to suffer. Can we imagine how much more relaxing life would be if we could expect and accept difficulty?

We harbour an irrational attachment to perfection and the availability of instant solutions. Western travellers often note how unflappable the locals seem in Third World countries when a three-hour train delay is announced, when none of the public phones work, or when crossing a road teeming with chaotic traffic. To a large degree, it is a matter of what we are used to, and in the West we believe the chorus from advertisers that we need suffer no discomfort, that there is a quick solution for every trifle. Yet wealth is not the answer to stress: philosophers have long observed that the excessively rich, arguably those in a position to stamp out every irritation, are likely to struggle even more with anger management than others.

When we wage a war against difficulty in all its forms and insist on our right to a smooth-running life, we can only end up frustrated by a losing battle. It sounds too obvious to even articulate but I will never be able to construct a life exactly to my liking. Yet if I look at my frustration throughout a typical day, this is exactly what I seem to have set my sights on. It is not that a Buddhist approach is about being passive in the face of difficulty or giving up. It is a matter of not allowing ourselves to become so emotionally caught up as we go about solving our problems.

Mother of two, Kerry, claims her main reason for trying to practise mindfulness and for squeezing some meditation into her week, is to provide perspective on all that happens throughout her day: 'when my practice is strong and I'm relatively present, it makes such a difference to my reactions. It's easier to accept setbacks and obstacles. I see them as normal and take them in my stride.'

The fact that life is difficult need not stop us from enjoying it. The Buddha is often misquoted as teaching, 'Life is suffering', but this is a grave mistranslation of his First Noble Truth, which is rather: 'There is *dukkha*, which is to be deeply understood.' A large part of understanding *dukkha* is seeing how we make most of it up, how we actively create it for ourselves through our habitually unskilful approaches to facing our difficulties. We protest against difficulty and we add what needn't be there.

Why am I so surprised when my day does not run to plan? Why am I so taken aback when people behave in a way I did not expect? I feel disbelief when the washing machine breaks down or when my computer misbehaves. We think we understand the Buddha's apparently simple teaching, that everything is impermanent, yet feel outraged to see this truth unfold in our own lives. So I must ask myself in times of stress, why should I alone be exempt from the universal law of impermanence?

One Zen practice is to meet each difficulty that arises with the gentle, non-judgemental words, 'And this.' So we cultivate a mind where, if milk is spilled at the dinner table, we say quietly to ourselves, 'And this.' We are running late for school: 'And this.' The school secretary phones to tell us our child is sick: 'And this.' We receive a speeding ticket or parking fine: 'And this.' It might sound like a far cry from our habitual way of reacting, yet with awareness of our options in any moment we can choose to calmly say, 'And this.' Such a reaction constitutes a 'letting go' and an end to any unnecessary suffering in our situation. This is what it means to 'wake up', a possibility available to us in any moment. If we feel ourselves incapable of saying, 'And this,' then we have an opportunity to investigate why and see what we are clinging to.

If we can expect that after taking reasonable care there will still be injuries, illnesses, breakages, spills, we feel less disappointed, less thrown by the inevitability of difficulty and imperfection. Any object we lose was impermanent all along, so maybe next time something breaks—a plate, a vase, a window—we could even consider feeling grateful for the time we were able to use it. Such a response is another example of letting go of habitual, unskilful reactions and 'waking up', a way to gain access to the freedom available in any moment.

If over the next few days you have any experiences of 'waking up'—experiences where you let go of any habitual tendency to snap, yell or panic—create a brief pause to examine your feelings.

The Third Noble Truth is: 'Suffering can end and that its end is to be realised.' That is, we need to pay close attention to the times when we have successfully managed to let go of craving or aversion. The deeper our experience of the peace of breaking free, the more motivated we feel to replicate the experience.

BE AWARE OF OUR 'SHOULDS'

We tend to cling to fixed ideas about how our days *should* turn out, about how others should behave, about how we ourselves should behave and how our lives should be. Then when life does not unfold according to our beliefs, we feel stressed, irritable and frustrated. Consider how much stress we have caused for ourselves by some of these beliefs:

- My children should take responsibility.
- My friends should make an effort to keep in contact.
- I should be more patient.
- My husband should appreciate me.

- It's sunny so I should be outside having a good time with all my friends.

Such aspirations are by no means 'wrong' or 'bad' and we could never stop them from arising in our minds, but the act of *clinging* to them—believing in them and insisting we fulfil them no matter the price—only creates anger, guilt and frustration with ourselves, our situations and with others.

Our aspirations become the voice of our inner dictator who pushes us around and does not care about our feelings. The overuse of 'should' in our thinking indicates unrealistic expectations and a reluctance to accept what is. We can still identify problems and strive to solve them, but inserting a 'should' is less than gentle, and usually harsh and judgemental. It signals an attachment to a view, and the Buddhist approach is to let go of any rigid clinging to views of how our situations should be. We need to notice our tendency to identify with our views—seeing each of them as '*my* view', defining, but also limiting, who I am—and dare to hold our views more loosely.

On one occasion, Camilla gently confronted me for using 'should' too often. She was questioning my tendency to start sentences with, 'As a Buddhist I should be more . . .' During our interview I asked her to explain her attitude to the word 'should'.

Everyone knows what they should and shouldn't do yet this is clearly not enough. In my view, obsession with 'should' leads to repression and in some cases extreme and even deviant behaviour. For mothers, it leads to guilt, which in turn creates a need to protect the self from judgement by others and ourselves. I've noticed that when 'should' has been too dominant in my life I'm more likely to criticise others as a way to avoid facing my own shame.

Before coming to Buddhism I was really trapped in that moral world of should and shouldn't, right and wrong. Notions of 'should' rely on my being a 'self' with complete control over my behaviour. Now, with Buddhist teachings, I'm finally seeing how important conditions are, for the Buddha taught that nothing happens in a vacuum: everything is utterly dependent on numerous causes and conditions. All my behaviour comes from preceding conditions, both within and outside me.

So say I'm tired and worn out, a child needs my attention and I lose it. I could say that I should not snap at that child but that would be ignoring the myriad conditions at play leading up to that moment, some of which I can control, many I can't. There are likely to be many to investigate but even if I can see the main ones, then I at least see matters more realistically as part of a series of never-ending processes. And that is more constructive than just feeling ashamed of myself.

So these days I find myself asking, 'What has caused this?' or, 'What preceded that?' or, 'Why is this coming up?' Rather than focusing on the fact that I snapped at the kids I can just apologise, explain that I was tired and move on. Perhaps more importantly, I can then take steps to change the conditions that led to the yelling. For example: going to bed earlier, being more present when I'm with the children, taking more care of an uncomfortable body or watching my thoughts and what I am telling myself.

Causes and conditions inform all our behaviour and we need to identify at least some of these clearly before we can fully take responsibility for ourselves. If we do not see how one of our beliefs, for example, habitually leads to a harmful action, why would we drop it? The problem is not 'wrong' thoughts so much as unacknowledged thoughts, those thoughts we fail to see and understand.

I should be more patient. I should be more organised. I shouldn't eat that cake. Often using the word 'should' only activates our inner rebel—we can't bear the pressure so it is simpler to disobey and do exactly what we 'should not'. A Buddhist alternative is to focus not on how inadequate we are but on cultivating non-judgemental awareness of our thoughts and feelings at such times.

When we practise Buddhist teachings we cannot help but perpetuate our habit of creating all kinds of new *shoulds* for ourselves: I've been meditating for fifteen minutes, I *should* be settled by now; I *should* feel more loving towards others; I *shouldn't* feel anger; I *should* be calmer. We host expectations of what should happen at this stage in our practice, at this stage in our meditation or at this stage on a retreat. We need to drop our expectations and open ourselves, non-judgementally to whatever is happening. I have found it is worth memorising the Chinese proverb: 'Tension is who you should be. Relaxation is who you are.'

RECOGNISE CONFLICTING DESIRES

Election night is coming up and part of me loves the idea of being at an election party where I would spend the evening with friends in front of the television watching the results come in. Another part of me feels tense at the thought that these friends might talk over the top of the coverage so I cannot hear it. I am in fact yet to be invited to an election party, but it intrigues me that I would both love and hate to attend one. On New Year's Eve, I need to feel that I have friends to spend it with, yet at the same time yearn for a quiet evening away from the hoopla.

The Buddha taught that desires are the cause of suffering, and one reason is that our desires are not only numerous but often conflicting. We see ourselves as a consistent self with certain fixed interests yet, as the Buddha taught, when we look more deeply we find no consistency of self and our so-called interests change from moment to moment. What does it mean for our lives that we play host to contradictory desires? We try to move in opposite directions at the same time and this is stressful. Our actions can be half-hearted. We have trouble committing. We feel confused about what we really want.

Back in 1926, Marion Milner, alias Joanna Field, started writing an illuminating journal, eventually published as the book, *A Life of One's Own*, a personal investigation into how she could find herself happiness. Although she was unaware of Buddhist teachings, her approach of throwing away the books, downplaying the advice of others and relying on her own direct experience is exactly what the Buddha taught us to do. Again and again, her discoveries on this journey chime exquisitely with Buddhist teachings.

She thought a useful starting point on her quest for happiness might be to come up with a statement of her main purpose in life, and to do this she listed some of her 'wants', only to discover:

I had thought I wanted a great many friends, but had often refused invitations because I hated to feel the beautiful free space of an empty day, free for me to do what I liked in, broken into by social obligations. I had thought I wanted to be a unique individual, but had been filled with shame when anyone disagreed with me, hastening to take back what I had said. I had thought I wanted to be importantly useful in the world, but avoided all opportunities for responsibility. I had thought I wanted to plumb human experience to the depths, and yet had striven to remain immaculately aloof from all emotional disturbance.

She discovered that her desires seemed confusingly contradictory. How do we choose which desire to follow, let alone our purpose in life, from amid such a mess? The answer lies in refusing to become a slave to our every desire, to become more aware of desires as they arise and to let go of the impulse to indulge quite so many of them.

Later in the book Joanna arrives at this point: 'I had begun to guess that my greatest need might be to let go and be free from the drive after achievement—if only I dared.'

With this discovery she was still free to strive for any of her personal goals, but less attached to any specific results of her actions. Throughout the book, Joanna notes occasions when she has been able to switch her habitual purpose-driven way of being in the world to one in which she drops all desire, such as in this example:

> . . . once when ill in bed, so fretting with unfulfilled purposes that I could not at all enjoy the luxury of enforced idleness, I had found myself staring vacantly at a faded cyclamen and had happened to remember to say to myself, 'I want nothing.' Immediately I was so flooded with the crimson of the petals that I thought I had never before known what colour was.

Her insights strike me as the Noble Truths in action: she discovers how desires and craving, even when they are fulfilled, fail to bring lasting satisfaction, and that letting them go and 'wanting nothing' leads to the end of the stress and suffering in any moment. So too, in meditation, when desires and craving finally quieten down for even a few moments, feelings of peace or even joy spontaneously arise.

Many question the Buddhist way: how do you get out of bed in the morning and motivate yourself to live your life if you want nothing? Yet the Buddhist path is not one of apathy and passivity, it is about holding our aspirations for our lives more lightly, taking them less seriously and not being so attached to particular outcomes. Joanna found this applied even during a game of ping-pong: the secret was to play not with a great frowning effort governing every movement but with a loose arm, physically relaxed and mentally unattached. She spoke of the need to psychologically 'stand aside'—or suspend that intense wanting of specific outcomes—and found this gesture valuable whether she was engaged in sewing, golf, tennis, drawing or singing.

If we watch closely we see that every moment of our days is punctuated by clinging and, its flipside, aversion, and that we tend to believe all our cravings are part of an unquestionable 'reality'. The tension in our bodies, the stress we feel in a typical day, is a response to the innumerable and often contradictory desires and impulses that arise. We wish the present moment was different to how it is. If our desires for our own lives are so rampant, we then multiply them by adding the urgent, desperate desires that modern parents hold for the lives of their children. (More about this in the next chapter.)

When we start to see the multitude of desires within us, we realise the need to cultivate awareness of their manic role in our lives: their potential to exhaust us, to mislead us and compound our suffering and stress. Desires will continue to arise in us but we cannot afford to take them all seriously. We need to be able to see them more clearly, label them, 'Oh, another desire is arising,' and let go, or not attach to them quite so much.

During times of discontent, when I see multiple and conflicting desires arising within me—mainly desires for my situation to be different from how it is—I remind myself of the Buddha's advice: 'Want little and know how to be satisfied.' Or I remember that wise expression: 'A man is rich according to his needs.' That is to say, needing little leads to a sense of abundance.

I believe I have actually made some progress when it comes to engaging less with arising desires. I am currently writing a biography for a man who wants to record his adventures for his grandchildren. He has led a racy, exciting life full of achievement, recognition and stimulation. As I listen to him I notice how he activates numerous desires in me: *I want that experience, that success, those fascinating friends, the travel, the attention.* Ten years ago, hearing his stories would have made me restless and dissatisfied with my life, vowing to make some improvements, but now I simply observe the various desires arising—sometimes even labelling them: 'another desire arising'—and let it go. These days I realise that none of these experiences will make me lastingly happy if I am incapable of happiness right here, right now.

By regularly practising gratitude and cultivating inner peace and contentment, our desires are more under control. Some Buddhists repeat to themselves: *Desires are inexhaustible. I vow to put an end to them.* I cannot quite believe that I would be capable of achieving such a state myself, but one experienced Buddhist assured me that, with practice, at least my desires would become more wholesome over time—and this I can believe. Still, this vow reminds me that most of my unexamined and innumerable cravings are no guide to how to run my life. Just as we 'choose our battles' with our children, we can try to choose the desires that we act on rather than responding to every one that arises.

We host conflicting desires within ourselves, but also within our families. Consider the example of a family of five—mother, father and three children—who find themselves on their long-awaited family holiday. It is the morning of day one and they have already reached an impasse: everyone has a completely different vision for the day ahead. Dad wants to go fishing, Mum wants to hire bicycles, one child wants to swim, another wants to stay and play in the holiday house and the youngest wants to buy ice-creams. They spend the next interlude negotiating and arguing and mopping up feelings of disappointment and reaching compromises. The same process repeats itself at dinner time as they all desire a different style of meal. Sound familiar?

Family life teaches us nothing if not the fine art of compromise. One of my friends—let's call her Kate—says her husband torments her with a long face for hours if he cannot implement his vision for the day and now it seems her eight-year-old son has inherited that very gene too. It is all too clear to Kate that the way her menfolk attach to their desires makes them suffer needlessly on the precise occasions when they could be at their happiest, such as a family holiday. Holding our desires more loosely, and being capable of letting go of our specific preferences, is key to a successful holiday—and a happy life.

CONSCIOUSLY RELAX

To bring my awareness back to my body and consciously release any tension has for me been a daily practice for years. I am often surprised, when I pay attention, at just how much tension has collected in my shoulders or face. My level of tension reaches a peak when I am rushing the children to arrive somewhere on time, but often too during certain daily episodes of small talk—running into somebody I half-know at the supermarket, entering a room of people I hardly know—times when I feel like I have nothing particularly interesting, helpful or witty to say. Georgina admitted to similar feelings:

> Perhaps I am an introvert but I sometimes feel very tense when I speak to other mothers while picking the children up from school. It is not that I don't like them, or that they are unpleasant in any way. I have just never enjoyed small talk, and with children interrupting and many mothers rushing off to after-school activities, small talk is all there is time for. There are days, of course, when catching up with my mother friends at school is the highlight of the day—it varies.

The school pick-up is especially tension-inducing when I need to rush off to swimming lessons and don't have time to talk to anyone yet find myself caught in a conversation. After a few years at a school, you know so many parents and you don't want to snub anyone so you have to acknowledge or greet everyone you know and make a split-second decision whether to stop for a chat. It feels like an over-attended party, if only brief—without the assistance of alcohol!

If we can identify the moments in our day when tension peaks, then we can stop any long-term build-up by allowing a moment to pause, breathe more slowly and relax our muscles. We can do this when we stop at traffic lights, stand in queues or wait for our computer to start—all times when our level of tension might rise further.

Our habitual way of living is to be miles away from our body, and the busier we are the less we stay in touch with how our body feels in the moment. The great advantage in returning our awareness to the body in times of stress is that the body is always here in the present moment, whereas the mind tends to ricochet around in time between various points in the past and future. Focused on the body and its sensations, we can halt a flow of unhelpful thoughts and worries. Our stories and dramas instantly drop away with this shift.

One of Joanna Field's discoveries in her quest for personal happiness was in the value of deliberately relaxing her muscles:

I soon found that knowing how to relax had other advantages besides improving my rest and my powers of perception. For instance, it acted like magic on those floods of irritation which are sometimes provoked by a particular person, an insistent mannerism, or some repeated distracting noise. Instead of narrowing my will to a fine point of exasperation—'Oh, why won't they stop it'—I found that

I could relax towards the distraction; instead of trying to push it away I could open my arms to it and let it do its worst. I found that even pain could be made bearable by this. I could also treat particular difficulties in my work in the same way.

Mental stress creates corresponding stress in the body. For some this is a knot in the stomach, others a lump in the throat, and for many a tautness across the shoulders. Subhana, a well-known Buddhist teacher in Sydney, suggests we identify the stress in our body, picture the location in our minds, focus our attention on the sensations there and breathe into that place to soften and release the tension. Again, this is a way to stop the circling thoughts and come into the present.

BREAK STRESS DOWN INTO ITS COMPONENT PARTS

The Buddha taught that every object, every phenomenon, every person is devoid of the 'self' we routinely assume to be there. All phenomenon are made up of component parts and each of these parts is the result of various causes and conditions. We can reduce a table, for example, to nails, glue, enamel and wood, and the pieces of wood to atoms, and so on. We cannot find a real 'table', but rather a stage in a process dependent on sun, trees, people, and our own minds that designate the object 'table'.

In the same way, what we usually see as our very own self is a collection of parts in process, reacting to all kinds of internal and external conditions. It is a convenient shortcut for us to see the world in terms of distinct, discrete objects and persons, but in doing so we overlook how reality truly is. This Buddhist teaching applies equally to our emotional states: they are made up of parts that are all in process, or changing into something else. What we call stress is made up of parts that might include complex combinations of shame, fear, resentfulness, guilt, shock, jealousy, panic, frustration or inadequacy. Hopefully not all at the same time.

The word 'stress' is amorphous, vague and lacking in shape. We see it in a fixed way without looking more closely at its component parts. We probably overuse the word 'stress' when other words might be more precise. Next time we feel stressed, try asking, what are the more specific emotions making up my stress, and even, what proportion of the overall feeling of stress does each emotion represent?

Samantha, a mother of two schoolchildren who I sat next to in a Buddhist workshop on emotions, feels stressed on seeing her children after school. In the workshop Samantha explored the emotions behind the stress.

> I know being reunited with my children is potentially a moment of joy and sometimes it is, but more often it does not work out that way. They seem to greet me with a string of demands which I usually need to deny them. They want friends to come over or they want to invite themselves over to someone else's house. They want me to spend money on them or give them a treat. Or they bicker with great vehemence.
>
> Looking closely, I can see the make-up of the stress that routinely builds in me. I would say that it is 30 per cent disappointment because I would like to see them smiling, hugging and pleased to see me. Another 30 per cent would be anger or irritation that they do not care about my feelings or about improving their behaviour. Ten per cent might be humiliation at other mothers seeing the behaviour of my family. And maybe the final 30 per cent is depression coming from my feelings of helplessness.

When we can name the various parts of this giant called stress, we gain some management of our state so we are less overwhelmed.

When we also acknowledge that each of these parts is in the process of transforming into another emotion, then we feel less trapped: the unpleasant emotion will not last forever, even though it feels like it might at the time.

Sharon Salzberg, in her book *Faith*, uses the metaphor of a musical chord which, in any musical score, is one sound made up of several notes. She suggests that we 'take apart the chord of our suffering' and identify each note. I have found this metaphor both beautiful and memorable. It has for me an almost magic way of transforming 'suffering' into a far sweeter 'melancholy.'

Planning

With so many details to manage, the mind of a mother has the potential to become irrevocably stuck in planning mode, which is not a particularly relaxed place to reside. Often we keep planning long past the point of decision-making—revising, tinkering round the edges and perhaps worrying about whether our plan is perfect enough. We may not realise that compulsive planning is addictive and can lead us to live in the future far more than we really need to.

Camilla developed some strategies to escape planning mode and help her live in the present more often:

In stressful times or when experiencing financial difficulties, I have found it helps to sit down and consciously make a plan or a budget. Once I've finished that process I stop thinking about it. Then if it comes up in my thoughts the next day I'll note, 'Hmm . . . I'm planning again,' but then resist the impulse to keep revising plans in my head. Even with our weekly schedules I use a calendar and sit down and plan out how the events are going, and then that's it: I don't need to concern myself any further. I write a lot more down because then I find I don't have to hold so much information in my head.

I used to think not having a plan meant I was more creative and spontaneous but routines in fact allow me more freedom because they free up mental space. With dinner, for example, it doesn't take very long to sit down and write out seven meals. I'm so tired after a day at work that the last thing I want to think about is what we are having for dinner. With a plan, I have shopped for everything and I don't have to spend all day wondering what to make and when I will have a chance to shop for ingredients. So my planning sessions help me live in the present moment more often.

Personally, I could never be that organised. I prefer to drop into the shops next to the boys' school every couple of days and avoid spending any time planning menus. Still, both of us have found ways to avoid living in planning mode, freeing ourselves to live in the present moment as often as possible.

•

Although the suggestions in this chapter mainly relate to our inner world, we can still work with our external conditions to some extent. We can reduce the stress of our lives by spending time in nature, making time for exercise, doing what brings us joy, and spending time with people who ground and inspire us. Making time for a Buddhist practice—by attending a group, studying the teachings, or meditating—is another way to remind ourselves that there is more to our lives than worldly achievements.

Inquiry

- Do you reject, suppress or deny feelings of stress or are you capable of simply saying, 'I feel stressed'?
- When you experience stress, what do you add, on top of the pure experience?
- Have you accepted that life, and parenting, will continue to present imperfection and difficulty or do you fight these at every turn?
- Does 'should' appear in many of your thoughts? What effect does it have? Does it help?
- Do you let your desires push you around? To what extent are you capable of observing them rather than acting on them? Can you see their often-conflicting nature?
- Do you pause throughout your day to consciously relax all your muscles?
- What are the component parts of your experience of stress? Is there also guilt, fear or anxiety?
- Do you spend too much time in planning mode? Are there practical measures that might allow you to free some mental space for presence?

CHAPTER 2

balance

WHAT IS IT ABOUT human beings that we have such difficulty settling for moderation? Life is difficult, so what do we do? We soothe ourselves by taking shelter at the endpoint of any spectrum, often dedicating our lives to an '-ism'. Some settle for hedonism, chasing pleasure and avoiding pain, others for workaholism, or we might opt for materialism, narcissism, alcoholism, fundamentalism or perfectionism.

Family life is no exception in this world of extremes. Our generation has been accused of 'extreme parenting'—of holding strong, inflexible views on how to parent properly. Yet extreme approaches do little to cultivate in us equanimity, contentment and inner peace. The unprecedented pressure today's mother endures, for example, to be a perfect mother, is unrealistic and has grave consequences for her capacity to be gentle towards herself. As Ita Buttrose and Penny Adams describe in their book *Motherguilt*, 'Today's mothers are suffering from an epidemic of guilt that is so powerful and so uniquely related to motherhood that it has its own name—Motherguilt!'

No fan of extremism, the Buddha taught the Middle Way. Prince Siddhartha Gautama, the man who would become the Buddha, grew up in luxury under a father who sought to protect him from the harsh realities outside the palace walls. When he finally explored the world outside, he witnessed the pain of birth, sickness, aging and death. Deeply troubled, he decided to find a solution to *dukkha*—which we tend to translate as suffering, stress or any form of unsatisfactoriness. Siddhartha spent six years living among matted-hair ascetics, fasting and generally depriving himself of all comforts (which was the done thing among spiritual seekers of the day), before realising that this had not brought him any closer to freedom from suffering.

By this point he had made two important discoveries: the extreme of self-indulgence that he experienced in the palace could never end *dukkha*; neither could the extreme of self-deprivation. In the Buddha's very first discourse after his enlightenment, and even before he presented his core teachings, he described his message as the 'Middle Way', the path between extremes.

Investigating our own experience of *dukkha*, we engage in finding the middle road, a road between ignoring unpleasant experiences and hating them. The middle road is one where we non-judgementally observe our experience with curiosity and openness. It requires us to face squarely the circumstances of our lives without escaping into unhealthy '-isms', addictions, obsessions or any of our numerous strategies designed to distract ourselves from pain. After all, have we not noticed how these habitual methods of escaping *dukkha* tend to create more of it?

The Buddha was radical: he taught that to end suffering, we do not suppress or ignore it but rather spend intimate time with it to examine exactly how it manifests and what causes it. This is the first of the Four Noble Truths: there is *dukkha*, which is to be fully understood. This means that when we suffer, whether it is mild irritation or crushing grief, we observe our experience closely in order to better understand exactly what is going on. This seems to go against common sense: how can investigating suffering relieve it? Surely the best solution is to keep ourselves distracted from any pain? Yet what we discover when we investigate *dukkha* in our lives is that the pain comes not so much from any adverse event itself but from our very attempts to block, deny and avoid the *dukkha*, or our habit of spinning egocentric stories about the *dukkha*.

It is a pretty typical afternoon *chez moi*: I have urged Zac to do his homework three times but he is still bouncing a ball against a wall. At least he has stopped arguing with his brother who has helped himself to the computer without my permission. Dragging Alex away from YouTube will take a battle but I'm behind on dinner preparation. Short on sleep, I'm feeling overwrought and capable of exploding any minute. Now is a perfect time to investigate *dukkha*, not on a cushion, but as I perform the simple, repetitive task of chopping dinner ingredients.

I consciously pause. I know that no matter how busy I am I can afford twenty seconds to return to my breath and bring my attention back to my body in the present moment. I notice tension all over my person: I am frowning, clenching my jaw and tensing the muscles in my back and shoulders. I relax and try to investigate the suffering. I notice the thoughts: *you shouldn't feel like this, stop being cross, I wish I could be happy and free of this emotional turmoil.* Yet this is aversion, an attempt to suppress my current experience, and it contributes significantly to my suffering.

I notice more thoughts: *When will the boys learn to take some basic responsibility for themselves? Why do I have to endure all this every day?* Yet in a state of conscious awareness I can observe these thoughts without engaging with them quite so much, without buying into them. There is no need to believe them as though they are any accurate representation of the truth. I try to be with my feelings, without changing them, curious, open and accepting. These feelings are a normal part of life. They come, they go, I accept them. I pay attention. Compassionate, non-judgemental attention. The act of being with my feelings, and accepting their existence, begins to subtly transform them.

If I practise mindfulness of the present enough I become familiar with my psychological patterns, the habitual ways of responding, that ensure the continuation of *dukkha.* Depending on who we are our patterns might include a tendency for self-pity, or martyrdom, or an insistence that everybody be just like me. Other damaging patterns might include tendencies for self-loathing, or the angry blaming of others without ever examining our own role. The Buddha teaches that when we fully understand how self-created our suffering is, we let go of the causes. We dispense with unhealthy extremes, with any toxic '-isms' and walk the Middle Way.

The idea of a Middle Way is helpful for mothers in regard to just about every issue we grapple with. Motherhood seems to require of us an avoidance of extremes: we would meet just as many problems if we were extremely strict as we would if we were extremely permissive. Our children will turn out troubled both if we ignore them or if we suffocate them with constant attention. We need to find a balance between exposing our children to the world and protecting them from it. We need to provide some entertainment and stimulation for our children, but not all the time. We need to be gentle, kind mothers—but not on those frequent occasions when we need to be firm and unyielding.

A mother's job is one of finding that middle road again and again, for all the various issues that arise, then change, then cease, making way for the next raft of issues to come along. For any matter we face, we always need to seek that point of balance and, once we find it, we need to be prepared to shift it to allow for changing conditions. We live in a world of flux and impermanence. The world outside us will continue to change, so any real stability and steadiness can only come from nurturing it within ourselves.

Whatever issue is currently on our radar—how much attention our children need, how often to see the neighbours—we find that the answer lies in creating conditions of balance. For example, I have wondered how much television is enough for sons who would happily spend half of each day in front of the box if I let them. Here is one answer I found in the book *Why TV is Good for Kids* by parents and media experts Catherine Lumby and Duncan Fine (although a more accurate title might have been *Why TV in Moderation is Not Particularly Harmful for Kids*):

> Balance is the key to developing well-rounded children who have a sense of their potential in many different areas. Like all activities,

television watching needs to be supervised by adults. It needs to be limited in a way that is age-appropriate and allows children time to do lots of other things.

In fact it is hard to think of an area in parenting where 'balance' is not the key, even the area of how much attention we give our children . . .

Balance in parental involvement

Today's parents have been accused of hyper-parenting, hothousing and too much hovering around our children. Author of *Parents Who Think Too Much*, Anne Cassidy, blames modern parents, including her former self, for creating in their children a condition she calls 'Attention Excess Disorder', or AED, where children habitually require 'large doses of parental attentiveness', such that they make 'not one request but scores a day'. She argues that our lives become overly child-centred, our children 'whiny, passive, self-centred and cheerless'. Now that in itself sounds a little extreme but we can all recognise multiple grains of truth in there, and feel our hopes rise when she adds that, 'kids left to their own devices . . . solve their own problems, develop inner resources and invent fantastic worlds'.

Maybe we should celebrate the recent state of affairs where children are more likely to suffer from excessive attention than neglect. Still, it is worth pondering the potential consequences of our own approach to ensure it constitutes a Middle Way. In Buddhist terms, some mothers of our generation risk an unhealthy attachment to their children informed by anxiety and insecurity about their parenting skills. Their relationship with their children has the potential to revolve more around the needs of their self-esteem—their need to see themselves as 'good' mothers—than a clear perception of what their children need. I often see such tendencies in myself: I catch myself rescuing, mollycoddling, fussing and *waitressing* for Zac, who is almost eleven, when it is high time he develops more independence. Yet motherhood can only be less enjoyable when it becomes another tool in our lives for self-evaluation.

Now that our children are older and are no longer so dependent, it is worth questioning ourselves occasionally: is it about time I went out alone with my husband? Am I pursuing some of my own interests in any regular, committed way? Have I cultivated genuine and satisfying friendships with people who are not family? Do I help people other than my own family? In answering such questions it is easy to adopt the norms of the mothers around us. Yet every school community has its own unique subculture, or several, that are worth identifying and in some cases guarding against. If, for example, those around us behave in an extreme way, hovering around their children and denying their own needs as mothers—or even the opposite extreme—we need to see this clearly and determine what is best for our own family, including ourselves. We may decide it is time to 'get a life', or even to scale down the one we have created.

We might exert excessive pressure on our children to achieve, supervise their every moment, monitor and pander to their every mood, or try to protect them from any form of suffering—all symptoms of being over-involved. Modern mothers are in such a habit of worrying whether they have given enough of themselves they rarely consider the pitfalls of the other extreme. There is no shortage of social commentators who believe the pendulum of parental involvement has swung too far, as we see from some recent book titles: *Hothouse Kids*, *When Will the Children Play?*, *Idolising Children* and *The Price of Privilege: How Parental Pressure and Material Advantage are Creating a Generation of Disconnected and Unhappy Kids*.

By scaling back on the amount of attention she once lavished on her three young daughters, Cassidy celebrates the discovery of a middle ground. After telling her daughters to 'leave us alone' so that she and her husband could finish their dinner in peace, she writes:

> Our girls are learning to wait their turn to speak. They play on their own and take care of each other. Because we are at their beck and call less often than we used to be, they turn more often now to books, to paper and pencil, to fantasy games. In other words, they, more than most kids I know, act like children.
>
> We haven't reverted to grunting communication in our house, nor do we ignore our children. But we have begun to assert our rights and create more balance in our family. I want our daughters to know that their father and I have our own inner lives, and that we have a life together as a couple. Our relationship with them is not all there is.

Cassidy also makes the thought-provoking point that the excessive levels of attention our children take for granted when they are young may not be sustainable for their parents in the longer term. That is, we could 'burn out' and potentially harm our children by withdrawing our attention too abruptly once they are older.

When their children announce, for example, that they are bored, many mothers fly into a guilty panic rather than let their children push through this emotion to that place where they find the inner resources to entertain themselves. Each child has a varying capacity to be resourceful, creative and imaginative when left to their own devices, and some mothers reap the rewards of granting some independence sooner than others. As any child psychologist will tell us, children need space to create their own childhood without relying on us to thoroughly structure their time and entertain them.

In my experience, children's ability to entertain themselves improves the more opportunities we allow them. I have just come through a long school holiday at home full of rainy days, but the boys have become so skilled at making their own play that the holiday was relatively painless compared to those of the past. Admittedly, my situation is possibly easier than that of others in that my sons make relatively compatible companions for each other, whereas other families might need to recruit friends and neighbours more often.

And who among us does not spare a thought for the freedoms of our own childhood? Most of us enjoyed the independence to roam our immediate neighbourhood and pursue adventures on bicycles or in nature, with a gaggle of other neighbourhood children. By the time we were school-aged, we probably spent hours each week without any adult supervision, most parents satisfied with only a vague idea of where we were and what we were doing. For many of us, these are the happiest memories of our lives. We might have engaged in some dubious activities, playing pranks and talking to the odd stranger (usually another child), but how ingenious we were in the invention of games and imaginary worlds. That world, for most families, is now extinct, but recalling it might spur us on to make a habit of leaving our children to play on their own or even judiciously shooing them away—without feeling any guilt.

Then there is the issue of how involved a parent should be in helping their children with their homework. Zac's school is one of several that have sent notes home to parents asking that they stop doing their children's homework for them. Psychologists are extremely concerned about parents helping too much with homework as it gives children the message that nothing they do by themselves is ever good enough. There are definitely occasions where some parental help is in order—in cases where the student is genuinely struggling or if the homework is beyond their capacities—but when a parent takes over school projects too often, the child's self-esteem can suffer.

Recently I listened to a radio segment about teenage depression in which a mother phoned in to plead with parents to stop helping their children so much. She explained that it took years for her daughter, who suffers from depression, to finally tell her mother that the constant helping made her feel inept. The poor mother was so distressed that all her good intentions had in fact been damaging.

Reflecting on the need for balance in how much attention I give my children has been liberating for me. If the children are playing well and the house is not in too much chaos, I can on rare occasions shut myself in a room to read, play the piano or meditate. I used to feel sheepish about such self-indulgent behaviour, seeing such times as 'bad-mother moments', but now I can see such treats for myself as sound mothering.

I remember one day, home alone with Alex before he had started school, I felt uneasy: I had been cleaning the house all morning and had not interacted with him at all. He was playing with some trucks and planes at his little table and I pulled up a chair and smiled at him: a picture of parental availability. He looked into my eyes and said, without emotion, 'Would you please go away, I'm trying to play my game.' Alex has always gone through patches of independence, but his request was illuminating: his life and his potential for happiness are not completely about me.

BALANCE IN OUR LIFESTYLES

For most of us, the area in our lives where balance is most threatened is in the pace we live at.

For mothers, there are usually such an overwhelming number of tasks to do in a day that we are in danger of becoming perpetually grim-faced and driven. At those times when I have become obsessed with my 'to do' list, I have glimpsed the potential to become quite a bore: someone who no longer makes time for friends, hobbies and hanging out with my family, someone who cannot afford to pause and take stock—or even enjoy a sit-down meal. My fuse is shorter and my outlook increasingly negative, since all I see are the obstacles on my mission to get things done.

Hopefully it is only temporary, but some of us lose the capacity to relax altogether: we might be on holiday but cannot seem to unwind and do nothing. Seeing a friend in the distance feels like a threat: our time is too valuable to give away for a chat. My friend Betsy used to be so driven that she kept breaking her toes on the furniture as she tore around her house. Her subsequent commitment to meditation, mindfulness and calming down has saved her mind and her feet.

We look at the sheer length of our 'to do' list and feel we have no choice but to be rushed and driven. But I have discovered an interesting tendency in myself to ignore the fact that not everything on the list needs to be achieved today. I crave the sense of completion that would come from crossing out every task yet this is a craving that leads to stress. When I make the effort to highlight the tasks that must be done today, my list is far shorter. It becomes manageable and I can relax into my responsibilities far more.

We need to recognise when we are attached to the prospect of 'getting it all done' because mothers can never arrive at this point, and if by some miracle they do, it won't last long if only because we need to keep our family fed. Curiously, the impossibility of achieving all we want in one day is another one of those truths we can see with our logical mind but which our behaviour does not reflect. Overambitious about what we can achieve today, we eventually find ourselves nursing an ongoing sense of failure that we never have everything under control.

I find meditation, whether it is one minute grabbed wherever or a formal sitting, an effective way to silence the more whip-cracking voices in my head. On the way to my cushion those voices will be yelling at me that I do not have time to sit, there are too many important things to do. Sometimes these voices barge right into my meditation, but they are only thoughts, not immutable realities, and as with any thoughts, I need not engage with them. Sitting on the cushion is my formal protest against becoming driven and stressed. Come what may, I will make time to relax and cultivate mindfulness, letting go of any attachment to the grand importance of my daily tasks. Even those of us who do not feel ready to commit to regular meditation can still insist on making time to pause and consciously relax for a few moments of every day.

We can also stop telling everybody how busy we are. This only feeds our frantic state of mind and wastes an opportunity for relaxing connection with others. We might even stop expecting others to be busy, as in, 'How are you? Busy?' I have heard people hint at disrespect for those who they see as not busy enough: 'What! She reads a book a fortnight! I would never have time for that. It's okay for some . . .' Consider bringing conscious awareness to your conversations on this point: do I have a need to impress on others that I am busy? Would I feel more relaxed if I stopped telling others how busy I am? Personally, I have made a vow that when people ask how I am I will never describe myself as 'busy'. It feels rebellious, counter-culture and quite relaxing too.

BALANCE IN OUR EXPECTATIONS OF OUR CHILDREN

As our children progress through each school year we need to deal with our expectations around their performance. Disappointments will arise often, for our children cannot be perfect, but how do we deal with our disappointments as well as our intense hopes? This can be the most critical question for even the most loving of parents for we are all in the position to do harm if we do not cultivate self-awareness of our expectations and their effects on our child.

Sigmund Freud described parental love like this: '. . . so moving and at the bottom so childish, it is nothing but the parent's narcissism born again.' He might sound scathing, yet who among us has not seen this theory in action? The stage-mother; the near hysterical father beside the sports field; the parents who organise hours of private tuition for play-deprived children. It is easy enough to see this parental narcissism in others but, if Freud is right, we all have some to face up to.

Some parents will not let anything stand in the way of their expectations of success for their children. On a Saturday in November 2007, an article of a highly unusual nature appeared on the front page of *The Sydney Morning Herald*, suggesting the presence of more than a few parental narcissists at one Sydney school. Journalist Gerard Noonan reported that Mitchell Donaldson, the school captain of an elite high school, had delivered an end-of-year speech to a packed assembly hall of over two thousand parents, teachers and students. This was not the speech that parents have come to expect on such occasions. For a large part of the twenty minutes he spoke, Donaldson lambasted a small but influential minority of parents who for years had bullied the school authorities to favour their children with prestigious positions and other forms of recognition.

Teenage boys have been forced to face up to the pressures of power-hungry parents. Those hypocrites who have slung the most mud do so because of a deep-seated sense of paranoia, inferiority and the unquenchable desire to social-climb. In a great paradox, these people are the embodiment of tall poppy syndrome yet all they crave is power. They accuse of intimidation, yet they are the biggest bullies of them all. They are selfish—because for every time their child is accommodated, another is displaced. They would never admit to doing so but must surely recognise it within themselves.

Just as parents who berate officials on the sidelines set a poor example, parents who undermine the authority of the school fail to recognise that life doesn't always deal in fairness, and you cannot excuse deplorable behaviour under the euphemism of wanting a 'fair go'.

Focused as this speech was on the damage such parents do the school community, we are left to imagine the harm they cause to their own children. At the conclusion of his speech, everyone in the room, including every parent—for there were obviously plenty of exceptions to the picture painted—rose to give him a standing ovation. Copies of the speech circulated around the various school communities, even becoming a text in other schools for the study of 'integrity'. My brother-in-law, now in his late thirties, had also attended an elite Sydney school, and at that Sunday's family barbecue assured me that this type of parent has always been around. He spoke in particular of the pressure they put on sports coaches to give their children the best positions, loudly and publicly criticising the incumbents.

These, of course, are the extremes. We might know a few such types personally but we certainly would not classify ourselves as part of this group. But is there any universal truth in Freud's words? We might all be, to varying degrees, parental narcissists, using our children to bolster our own egos, fetch us glory and make us feel good about ourselves. To what extent do we, with all our expectations for our children, get in the way of their process of becoming their own person? We might, for example, cling to strong views, biased by our own experiences, about what makes a person worthwhile. In some families it will be musical ability, others sporting prowess or popularity, but the most common expectation of our time is for children to be high academic achievers, and for this they need to be intelligent.

We all know someone for whom intelligence is the key to having any worth as a person. Such characters pride themselves on 'not suffering fools gladly'. They often refer to someone they have met as an 'idiot', a 'goose' or a 'clueless moron' who has 'no idea what they're doing'. Disrespect for others, based on a perceived lack of intellect, characterises most of their conversation. While such characters are definitely in the minority, their attitudes are still contagious, for often we base our respect for others on how intelligent we perceive them to be, undervaluing other aspects of their character. So as parents we risk insisting our children prove their intelligence, hence their worth.

Attachment to the need to be intelligent and, in particular, for our children to be intelligent, overlooks the fact that intelligence can sometimes lead to great harm. It is not always harnessed for making the world a better place. The daily news is full of examples of educated professionals and politicians using their intelligence for the purposes of intimidation, corruption and cruelty. Many Nazis were highly intelligent and well-educated, not least the doctors who conducted cruel experiments on Jewish children. And no matter how intelligent someone is, they might not always choose to use their intelligence, and without inspiration their intelligence is wasted.

I was once writing a biography for a client with a renowned intellect and a rather lordly demeanour. I was a little intimidated by him at first and told my friend Anne as much in an email. She sagely wrote back, 'Ah yes, but does he have emotional intelligence?' What a good question, I thought. After all, those who have made their life's work the study of emotional intelligence—the ability to monitor one's own and others' feelings—have found it to be a much more reliable predictor of success in life than the conventional intelligence quotient. Anne's email reminded me to stop over-valuing a person's intelligence quotient.

Even in Marek's world of engineering, where cognitive ability is highly valued—as it should be—many technically competent engineers will nevertheless not be hired as they lack the ability to work with others, to lead, or to relate skilfully to clients. Our world needs people with cognitive intelligence, emotional intelligence, social intelligence, practical, street-smart intelligence, and on the list could go. Most of all, our world needs people with good hearts, to remind us all of where and how to invest our energy. As I write, the world's financial markets are collapsing, creating worldwide anxiety and insecurity, for the simple reason that some of the world's brightest minds aspired to nothing higher than filling their own hip-pockets, rather than using their intellect to ease suffering in the world or make it a better place for others.

I have to put up my own hand at this point and plead guilty to a life-long overvaluing of intelligence. In my case, though, this has been fuelled by anxiety over whether my own intellect is quite lofty enough. I attended a selective high school where I felt myself to be surrounded by my intellectual superiors. With so many brilliant and amazing girls around me, opportunities to shine were rare. I often wondered how I ever managed to qualify. (Was it because my mother had done so much voluntary work at my primary school and this was their way of thanking her?)

Interestingly, some of my former fellow high-school students today feel bitter about their experience of being at a selective school and about the effect it had on their self-confidence. A few I have spoken to would never send their own children to one. Yet thousands of parents do overlook these self-esteem issues and subject their children to hours of coaching so that they can enter a selective school. While a selective school may suit a great number of children, even among the very bright students, there are exceptions.

I could easily have become a mother who pressures her children for academic excellence, in response to my own anxieties and ego needs. I am fortunate to have had the opportunities to be educated out of such an approach. These days I make a point of praising the boys' *efforts* rather than dwelling only on their results. All they can do is their best.

BALANCE IN OUR EXPECTATIONS OF OURSELVES

Sophia, whose children I was minding during some school holidays, arrived to pick them up one afternoon with a tear-stained face. Not the type to hide her feelings, she explained to me that she had spent the past two hours crying yet could not identify why. We talked for a while and eventually she attempted to diagnose her problem: 'I guess I just feel like I'm not doing anything well.'

The school holidays had been particularly testing for her: 'Yesterday I took the children out in the morning and again in the afternoon, and by evening they were complaining that I wouldn't take them out for dinner as well.' Sophia is a full-time professional who always looks spectacularly well-groomed and consistently presents an immaculate house. I asked her whether she was a perfectionist and her answer was, 'Definitely.' We talked a little longer and I urged her to consider lowering her expectations of herself—I also slipped her a couple of magazine articles about the benefits of allowing our children to be bored occasionally during the school holidays.

Any psychologist will tell us that among the mothers most vulnerable to depression are the perfectionists. Striving for perfection, both at work and at home, in an attempt to please everyone all the time, is not only exhausting but impossible. When we fail to meet our unrealistically high expectations, feelings of guilt can invade our lives. Perfectionists in particular need to work on creating an unconditionally loving relationship with themselves. Meditation is useful for enhancing our ability to take a step back from the voices of our inner critic, our inner slave-driver or bully—theirs are not the voices of truth. We have the choice to take them far less seriously, if not ignore them altogether. Meditation is the practice of this very skill: meeting whatever arises during a sit with calm, non-judgemental awareness, or what Buddhists call *equanimity*. While we practise equanimity during meditation, the idea is to bring it, as often as possible, into our daily lives.

A Buddhist antidote to guilt involves seeing our situation clearly and finding a point of balance between taking full responsibility for any mistakes or inadequacies on the one hand and self-flagellation on the other. A degree of remorse can be an excellent source of learning but guilt is different. Guilt goes on and on, without resolution and without compassion for ourselves. In the interests of clear-seeing, we might also practise conscious awareness of any unhelpful beliefs that feed our guilt: *I must always look my best*; *My house should always be tidy*; *I must never make mistakes*; *My children should always be happy and loving and never bored or irritable*; *I must please everybody all the time and never let anybody down*.

Although our 'inner critic' provides so much of the fuel for our guilt attacks, she is just one of many competing voices in our heads and, like any of these voices, we do not need to take her word for everything. She is not always as smart as she thinks she is. We certainly dislike our 'inner critic' and, as we do for anyone who criticises us, blame her for making us feel sad. Yet sometimes she has something useful to say and, like some of the difficult people we have met, her main problem is in her tone of voice or the way she delivers her message. As I edit and polish this manuscript, my inner critic is my greatest asset, helping me to improve my language and mercilessly slash paragraphs that might have bored readers. Rather than slay her, what we need is to make peace with our inner critic and, if she gives us a hard time, tell her to use more sensitive language and a more compassionate tone.

So the solutions to guilt, in its more festering forms, are to lower our expectations, to foster gentleness and patience towards ourselves, and to take the more bullying voices in our heads less seriously. We call a truce with our inner critic and commit to constantly forgiving ourselves for not being Wonder Woman.

BALANCE IN AFTER-SCHOOL ACTIVITIES—OR NOT...

I feel like a fool. Having just written a chapter about the importance of balance and the avoiding of extremes, my son Zac, who has been doing two hours of gymnastics for the past couple of years, has just committed to a new regimen at a new club. Here's the rub: it requires twelve hours a week. I felt exceptionally nervous about the decision to sign up, a decision affecting three days of our week. Where was the balance in such a commitment?

Zac is tireless as a nagger and insisted that gymnastics was his passion and this was what he wanted to do no matter the sacrifice. And what a sacrifice twelve hours is. He has had to give up soccer, which he has been enjoying for years. He will have less time for school work, less time for unstructured play, for seeing his friends, for piano practice (I admit, that's my passion more than his). His days will be packed. *My* days will be packed since I am the schmuck driving him to the new gym a few suburbs away. He will be so tired.

What a lot of mental space decisions about activities—be they musical, sporty or social—can take up for a parent. I am by no means the only parent facing the decision whether to specialise according to a child's talents or provide a wider range of experiences to raise a 'well-rounded' individual. The choices of after-school activities these days are so abundant that indecisive parents, among whom I count myself, can find themselves in a real lather.

The decision to quit an after-school activity can also be a difficult one, especially after we have invested so much time and money not to mention our fantasies about future delights if our child excels. At what point are we being a pushy parent when we insist our child continues an activity they suddenly dislike? No expert, no book, no generalisation can advise us, as the answers to such conundrums always depend on the individual child.

I have to admit, the words 'well-rounded' have been a theme in many of my parenting decisions. Yet for all my hand-wringing, Zac took the decision out of my swollen hands, by coming home from school recently and telling me he had informed the sports master of his decision not to play Saturday soccer for the school as he was switching to gymnastics. The sports master apparently yelled at him, and two other boys who made similar last-minute decisions, for half an hour. Unfazed, Zac had made up his mind and, as much as I felt tempted to, I could not stand in his way. He had set fire to a bridge.

Only a few pages back I extolled the virtues of 'balance in our lifestyles'. I have written whole-heartedly about the need in children for unstructured time, free from pressure and hothousing. Yet maybe it's time for me to step aside and allow Zac some rights to manage his own life. Maybe this is the Buddhist practice of non-attachment when it comes to our children: allowing them the freedom to grow into their own person. My fingers are crossed for Zac that his choices will make him happy, and like all mothers who have to let go, I will probably not uncross them for the rest of my life.

Inquiry

- How do you cope with the difficulties of life—and parenting? Are any of your strategies arguably 'extreme'?
- How involved are you in your children's lives? How much attention do you give them? Have you found the point of balance? Do you consider shifting that point as conditions change over time?
- Have you cultivated enough self-awareness to recognise when you are overly driven?
- Are you aware of your own expectations for your children and any possible effects?
- Have you managed to create a peaceful relationship with your 'inner critic'?
- Do you practise non-attachment by allowing your children, particularly older children, to make some of their own decisions?

CHAPTER 3

boredom

SOMETIMES FOR MOTHERS, THE repetitive nature of the daily routine—doing the school run, attending to the demands of after-school activities, providing a hot meal—wears us down and we find ourselves dissatisfied. There must be more to life than this, we tell ourselves. Words like 'drudgery', 'daily grind' and 'monotony' float through our minds. Gradually, we can lose our ability to be content. We might start craving holidays, career changes, affairs or consumer goods, and these may seem like effective solutions—at least for a while. Occasionally we simply need more time for ourselves and, while we can often take measures to spice up our lives, sometimes the real problem is the state of our minds.

HANOI, HERE WE COME!

Winter has landed in Sydney. My house is as cold as an igloo, and when temperatures are low I struggle to keep my spirits high. Somewhat seasonally affected, I sorely miss the sunshine and start to find my life lacking and boring—each day seems exactly the same as the last. My thoughts turn to escape fantasies: I need to move somewhere warmer. Sydney, of course, is a relatively warm city, but as Polish Marek points out, this means we lack the experience of Europeans in insulating our buildings. His overseas family shiver their way through their visits to Sydney, our heating systems no match for the general absence of double-glazing.

A friend emails me an advertisement about an opportunity for ten writers to live in various cities of Asia for four months. Could this be what I am looking for? I had always wanted to go to Vietnam, so I prepare an application proposing I take the boys—they could always attend the international school—and do a spot of travel writing. At least next year I might be warm through winter, not to mention stimulated by an exciting new project. I make a promise that I will not allow myself to become attached to the idea but it is already too late. I am obsessed right from the get-go. I start learning Vietnamese, studying the region's history and geography, and telling everybody I meet about my plans. I wonder how I will survive the six months it will take the panel to make their decision, let alone how I will cope if my application is rejected.

There are other problems too. Marek would have to stay in Sydney for work, and when I tell him about my application his exact words are: 'Over my dead body.' Marek is the type who needs to be within touching distance of his loved ones and I can appreciate his viewpoint. Still, he had enjoyed many weeks of travel with his sports team when Zac was a baby. They had been difficult weeks for me, so I figure a little sacrifice on his part is only fair. I would try to persuade him, two minutes each day, presenting the case for an overseas jaunt for the boys and me. He could always fly up for a visit? I have to admit, however, that my case almost collapsed whenever he asked, 'How can you justify the cost of the international school fees up there?'

A few weeks pass and then Marek receives an email at work that beggars belief. The Hanoi office of his company urgently needs an engineer for a week—immediately. Marek never receives emails like this, so imagine our surprise. Of all the cities in the world, they want Marek to go to the exact one we had been discussing on a daily basis. All four of us could fly up and stay in Marek's hotel. It would be a perfect opportunity to assess Hanoi as a place for a longer stay.

Even still, Marek assures me before we set off that there will be nothing of interest for the boys and that, aged six and nine at the time, they will be too young to appreciate the experience. Alas, he is wrong. Alex in particular savours the constant adulation the Vietnamese lavish on him as a blond child. Both boys relish travelling by the pedal-driven cyclos, the outdoor markets with their live crabs, eels and lobsters, and all the fascinating military history. They are reluctant for the trip to end.

By the end of the trip I feel grateful at the chance to have shared a precious experience with the boys and more than a little surprised that my need to move to Hanoi had begun to wane. Through contacts at Marek's work in Hanoi, we had learned more about what life would be like if we lived there. One of Marek's colleagues, a Vietnamese father who had once lived in Sydney, lamented how his young sons miss out on all the organised sport we take for granted in Australia. It simply does not exist in Hanoi: they don't have the fields, the open spaces or the volunteers who can organise a program. How would Zac and Alex release their considerable energy? I want as much of their childhood as possible to be spent on grass, on earth, in nature. Kindly showing my family around, our contact took us to a noisy video-game arcade where his children spent 'most of their childhood'. I could not leave the arcade quickly enough: I wanted cultural experiences, not this.

What clinches my turnaround, however, is the motor-scooters. Hanoi is the motor-scooter capital of the world; cars are rare in comparison. The streets of Hanoi are a sight to behold, thick with scooter traffic carrying babies, toddlers, elderly grandparents and families of four—with barely a helmet in sight. A great novelty for tourists, the motor-scooter traffic would be hard to live with over the longer term. Crossing the street with two children is one of the most stressful exercises imaginable. On one occasion I was crossing the street, believing Alex was next to me when he was, in fact, dawdling two feet behind. A motor-scooter skidded noisily, missing him by an inch. It took me hours to recover.

Boredom and dissatisfaction often come from blindness to our own wealth. We moan about traffic and parking conditions in our large cities, forgetting how much worse they could be, or how much worse they are in most other big cities in the world. Weekend sport commitments might feel like an onerous duty at times, denying our right to a weekend, but what a miracle that there are so many hundreds of volunteers out there to organise, coach and manage the thousands of children who play each weekend. What wonderful, healthy memories we create for our children by playing our part in this community.

As for my aversion to winter, the Buddha did address our tendency to hold strong seasonal preferences, with these words:

Those whom summer's heat tortures
yearn for the full moon of autumn
Without even fearing the idea
That a hundred days of their life will then have passed forever.

Yes, hating the season is a form of wishing your life away. And life is already so short.

As with many of my contemporaries, I have romanticised travel as some great ideal. In my early twenties, suffering from 'anywhere-but-here' mentality, I even used to judge a person's worth by how much travel they had 'achieved'. Yet with age and experience, I became disillusioned by the lack of authenticity of many travel experiences. Travelling, while often eye-opening and rewarding, could also be a commercialised and contrived experience far removed from the reality of local life.

Besides, what was to say that a traveller could not be dull and shallow in their outlook, or a stay-at-home content and profound? The state of one's mind, wherever one finds oneself, will always be more important than what country one is in. This is why Zen Buddhist doctor, father and author Jon Kabat-Zinn called one of his books *Wherever You Go, There You Are*. No matter how far we travel, we bring all our old patterns, all our habitual ways of interpreting our surroundings, along with us.

I also began noticing how people, not least myself, used travel experiences to enhance a fabricated sense of identity as a worldly, experienced adventurer, proudly telling others: 'This necklace is from Egypt,' or 'When I was in Hanoi, I . . .' It took me a few years to admit to myself: *where I have been is not who I am.*

After our trip to Hanoi, I started wondering how I had managed to delude myself so completely. Why had I thought that living overseas would cure my winter blues? I had been searching outside myself for satisfaction, ignoring that Hanoi would present just as many, if not more, irritants in daily life. In reality, I could only work with myself. So back to the meditation cushion for me.

In the months that followed our trip I enjoyed an enhanced appreciation for the safe, healthy childhood I am able to provide my children in Sydney. I even enjoyed the traffic, knowing, *this is nothing!* December finally arrived, bringing the letter announcing the panel's decision. With perfect nonchalance and non-attachment, I opened it. My application was . . . unsuccessful. I threw it in the garbage bin and jumped straight in the car to take the boys for a swim. Marek would be relieved at the result. I did not admit my true feelings to him, but so was I.

GRATITUDE

Camilla floored me once by saying she loved housework—an activity with which I still struggle to reconcile myself. (The sheer amount! The unequal distribution of labour! All the things I'd rather be doing!) Apart from seeing it as a chance to practise mindfulness, she also brings large doses of gratitude to the process.

I had a very difficult home life as a child with an alcoholic father, so that created a condition in me to value a home that people want to be in and that I can share with friends. The home, for me, is a real sanctuary. I feel very blessed to have a family and a house that runs smoothly. A family home is a gift of immense value and deserves care and attention, so without becoming obsessive about housework I just throw myself into it.

And her gratitude does not end there. She continues:

I wish all the world's problems were as simple as housework because with housework you get a result. Compared to really difficult world problems or even problems with our children's behaviour, the solutions for housework are very immediate. I have this whole load of dirty dishes: I wash them and here they are all clean. I find sweeping fantastic in this way because I appreciate the simplicity.

The happiest people I know are the ones who know to be grateful. For a lucky few, gratitude comes naturally for they can clearly see how much there is to be grateful for. Social workers, health professionals and other service-industry workers sometimes have a headstart in any practice of gratitude for they are in constant contact with those who face the most difficult challenges and who constantly remind them of how blessed their own lives are. Others with an edge are those who have experienced extreme forms of suffering—a family breakdown, an illness—and can now enjoy a more peaceful stage of life.

My experience writing biographies for clients to share with the younger generations of their families has put me in contact with a wide variety of people, including a Jewish man who survived the Holocaust and lived to eventually derive immense pleasure from the simple act of gardening. Like other Holocaust survivors I have heard about he lives in gratitude for the gifts of the earth. Having suffered so profoundly, he savours the peacefulness offered in an intimate relationship with nature. After many hours of recording the memories of this client, it was heart-warming to see his face beam as he reported: 'I realised my dream with a garden of 140 roses! I grew many other plants and even received a prize from the Society for Growing Australian Plants.'

Even if gratitude does not come naturally to us and we are more likely to spot what is wrong or missing in our lives, we can still choose to intentionally cultivate gratitude. Any one of us can take a few moments each day to pause and appreciate unconditionally the gift of our own precious life. The Tibetans would express it as 'a precious human rebirth'. We can initiate a habit of counting our blessings at least daily. We can open our eyes to how the rest of the population of the world lives and understand that we lack little in comparison. We can acknowledge that everything we have comes from our environment or from other people and that we are nothing without our interconnectedness to others. Gratitude fuels generosity and increased connectedness to everyone we deal with.

I did not enjoy my first day working in the canteen at Zac's new school. After five straight hours of kitchen duties, I could easily have fallen into resentment about the prospect of repeating this day four more times that year. I could have thought about the mothers who can help, but don't. I could have wondered why fathers manage to avoid such duties. I could have questioned why the school does not pay me for such tiring work. To be honest, I did all these things. But I also decided not to wallow there and the best mechanism for rescuing me from the bad karma I was creating was gratitude.

Only by remembering how fortunate I was—to be part of a cohesive community of volunteers, to have my son at a school where he was happy and the teachers worked hard—could I begin to give my time with a more loving heart. I could be grateful about the abundance of food available for our children, the bravely cheerful mothers around me, the politeness of our young customers—and the fact that I was not one of the permanent members of the canteen staff.

Gratitude is the fast-track to contentment. The Buddha taught that craving is the cause of suffering, so gratitude for what we have is an effective antidote to craving what we do not. We naturally slow the perpetual stream of wanting when we see that our cup is already so full. For this reason, many Buddhists make counting their blessings a formal part of their meditation sitting, aware of the role of gratitude in countering the craving that leads to suffering.

Since gratitude is such a powerful state of mind, it is worth cultivating it in our children. In Chapter 6, we look at ways to teach our children to be grateful for what they have but I find a cosy bedtime activity is to literally count our blessings, and acknowledge anything we appreciate about our lives. The three of us brainstorm ideas together and there are no wrong answers. Or sometimes, if I am enjoying nature with my children, looking at a sunset, watching the waves of the ocean, or enjoying a view, I might say to them, 'Isn't it great to be alive?' I hope that this models for them the possibility of feeling thankful, not just for material blessings, but for life itself or as Tibetans tend to put it, 'the gift of a human life'.

OVER-RELIANCE ON SENSORY STIMULATION

Buddhist teacher Christopher Titmuss in his book *Light on Enlightenment*, an introduction to the main Buddhist teachings, talks about the habit of trying to stimulate our senses as a way to overcome boredom:

... we have become beggars at the sense doors and slaves to the endless pursuit of pleasurable sensations through our eyes, ears, nose, tongue and touch to relieve the way we slug along in everyday life. We imagine the whole reason for existence is maximising the number of pleasurable experiences and minimising the unpleasant ones. Yet making this our primary aim actually invites countless unpleasant states of mind and we eventually get bored with this pursuit too.

This quote explains the reason why many of us became parents: we became bored with our lifestyle of trying to keep ourselves entertained. The pursuit of sensory pleasures that characterised our pre-children days—the restaurants, the cinemas, the various social gatherings—started to feel, for many of us, meaningless and unsatisfying. Parenthood can symbolise a readiness to grow up and leave the life of pleasure-seeking behind. Of course, parenthood is not the one and only way of reaching maturity, but it definitely forces a degree of selflessness upon us.

Yet even as parents, when boredom sets in, we might return to our habitual ways of waiting at the sense doors for happiness. An extramarital affair offers those with any energy left over after the demands of family life not only relief from feelings of boredom but also a chance to defy the aging process by assuring themselves they are still attractive. In an article in *The Sydney Morning Herald* entitled 'Let's talk about sex, ladies', journalist Jane Sullivan reports on a recent survey of two thousand women. Although she suspects that the sample was more sexually active than the general population, she writes:

One woman in five has had an affair but most aren't happy about it. They feel guilty, dirty or depressed. 'It was the worst thing I

have ever done in my life and it ruined everything good that I
had,' says one 29-year-old.

The main reason women give for cheating is apparently 'boredom';
men, 'opportunity'. In the Ask Sam blog on sex, dating and relationships,
Samantha Brett cites writers such as Deidre Sanders and Mira
Kirshenbaum who have each done extensive surveys on why people
cheat, Kirshenbaum claiming, 'it's a combination of boredom, dull sex
and no conversation that pushes women to do it'. Sanders reports based
on her study of 10,000 respondents: 'Some 64 per cent of men said it
was because they had the opportunity while 60 per cent of women said
it was more exciting and because they wanted someone to talk to.'

Writers Kylie Ladd and Leigh Langtree have compiled an
anthology called *Naked: Confessions of Adultery and Infidelity*, where
24 contributors, writing from a diverse range of situations, share their
experiences of the effects of unfaithfulness. While most of the women
who participated in affairs eventually regretted it, this was not the
case among the seven mothers in the sample. While only two of these
affairs lasted over the long term, four of these mothers—including
two in happy marriages—felt they ultimately benefitted from their
decision to be unfaithful.

From a Buddhist perspective, however, the hazard with affairs is
that they are yet another attempt to find happiness outside ourselves.
We relegate to somebody else the power to make ourselves happy,
forgetting the importance of our own minds in addressing our pain,
whether our pain be loneliness, boredom or fear of aging. While many
women have come to scoff at the idea that a man could deliver lasting,
reliable happiness, plenty continue to pursue the dream.

One of the Buddha's precepts, or ethical guidelines, along with not
stealing and not killing, is not engaging in sexual misconduct. Those
wishing to present this precept in more positive language translate it

as 'practising contentment'—the result of letting go of desires. Given his words as presented in the classic Buddhist text *The Dhammapada*, we can assume sexual misconduct includes adultery:

> Adultery leads to loss of merit, loss of sleep, condemnation and increasing suffering. On this downward course, what pleasure can there be for the frightened lying in the arms of the frightened, both going in fear of punishment? Therefore do not commit adultery.

Although 'loss of sleep' would be the greatest deterrent for me, the Buddha heads the above list of negative consequences with 'loss of merit', which means those who stray lose some of their access to any good karma they have created in the past—which makes sense given the number of new problems they are likely to confront.

At the risk of digressing, I have to admit to feeling a little uncomfortable at the Buddha's words above for it is not beyond my imagination to conjure scenarios where adultery is not so harmful. In fact, one of the more prominent Buddhist couples in the United States have had sexual relationships outside their marriage, which apparently harmed nobody involved, according to the wife's published memoir. Fortunately, there is always a loophole when we find any Buddhist scriptures disturbing, as the Buddha said, 'Do not be satisfied with what has come down in the scriptures', for he advises us to 'know in yourselves' what avoids harm. (We explore this quotation more thoroughly in the next chapter.) While ethics, responsibility and honesty are of primary importance on a Buddhist path, it is still a path capable of recognising the complexity of each individual case rather than applying blanket rules to every situation.

Maybe I should give the last word to the Venerable Thich Nhat Hanh, drawing from his Fourteen Mindfulness Trainings. These

Trainings are Thich Nhat Hanh's attempt to combine the Buddha's precepts as well as his Eightfold Path, in a way that reflects modern-day concerns. (I found them so inspiring, such a statement of how I would aspire to live, that I stuck them on the wall next to my bed to revisit regularly. The full list is in the Appendix.) His Fourteenth Mindfulness Training is specific about how best to avoid the harm that comes from sexual misconduct:

> Aware that sexual relations motivated by craving cannot dissipate the feeling of loneliness but will create more suffering, frustration, and isolation, we are determined not to engage in sexual relations without mutual understanding, love, and a long-term commitment. In sexual relations, we must be aware of future suffering that may be caused. We know that to preserve the happiness of ourselves and others, we must respect the rights and commitments of ourselves and others.

The senses provide fleeting pleasure, but not lasting happiness. We need to attack the causes of our boredom, and Christopher Titmuss has a clear idea of what these might be:

> It is common enough knowledge that living without awareness generates dullness as a side effect . . . We need the practice of developing our consciousness to go from gross desires to subtle appreciations in daily life. If it were our last day on earth would we feel bored? The grip of boredom takes away appreciation and love for the ordinary.

What helps many seekers to live more in the present is taking that traditional advice where we try to live every day as if it were our last. After all, one day it will be.

Cultivating perplexity

One of the most interesting teachers in the world, according to many Buddhists I know, is Stephen Batchelor. He has written several books about Buddhism and his many articles and talks are all over the internet. He offers an interesting perspective in that he is a highly experienced practitioner in all three of the main Buddhist traditions, having lived as a monk in Tibet, Korea and Switzerland before 'disrobing' and founding a retreat centre in England.

He can be a controversial figure for he is committed to challenging the need for any religious trappings in the practice of Buddhist teachings. His emphasis on the importance of 'perplexity, unknowing and mystery' in our practice suggests a radical way of being in the world that is a far cry from any state of boredom. Here are some of his insights from the book *Buddhism Without Beliefs*, in a chapter entitled 'Freedom'. He describes a radical approach to 'ordinary' objects and phenomena:

> As soon as awareness finds itself baffled and puzzled by rainfall, a chair, the breath, they present themselves as questions. Habitual assumptions and descriptions suddenly fail and we hear our stammering voices cry out: 'What is this?' Or simply: 'What?' or 'Why?' Or perhaps no words at all, just '?'

This is a type of questioning that young children model perfectly for us. Little children are fully plugged into the present moment because of the natural enjoyment that flows from their curiosity. Batchelor explains an important aspect of perplexity:

> The questioning that emerges from unknowing differs from conventional inquiry in that it has no interest in finding an

answer . . . It recognises that mysteries are not solved as though they were problems and then forgotten. The deeper we penetrate a mystery, the more mysterious it becomes.

What a relief to feel no pressure to find an answer. We can say to ourselves, for example, *I don't know who I am and that doesn't matter*. As soon as we feel we *should* know, we lose our freedom. Batchelor continues:

Perplexed questioning . . . prevents the quality of awareness from becoming a passive, routinised stance, which may accord with a belief system but renders experience numb and opaque. Perplexity keeps awareness on its toes . . . Questioning is the track on which the centred person moves.

Fired with intensity, but free from turbulence and the compulsion for answers, questioning is content just to let things be.

According to Batchelor, our questioning need not be intellectual, analytical or even particularly specific. It is about seeing every moment of our lives as part of an ever-unfolding mystery. Free of any attachment to goals, purposes and ego-needs, we feel ourselves become more alive, more awake and less bored.

If we lose our capacity for perplexity, for questioning and wondering, we start to freeze our perceptions of others, of ourselves and of our children. We start perceiving those around us as permanent, unchanging and separate. It is especially unrealistic to inflict this tendency on our children, for they are growing and changing and interacting constantly in a school environment different from the one we experienced in our own childhoods. This means we can never take who they are for granted and need to observe them with fresh eyes on a daily basis. The most accurate way to perceive each of our children is as an ever-unfolding mystery. With minds thus oriented, we are more likely to listen closely when they speak to us and meet them with presence and openness.

It is human nature to want to label our children as certain types of people: 'timid', 'adventurous', 'social', 'helpful'. Labels help us to simplify infinite complexity, which can be useful to a point, but labels also limit our perception of our children and shape the way we interact with them. When Alex was at pre-school he gained a reputation as wild and naughty. A teacher took me aside and expressed concern about his readiness for school: mentally he was up to the challenge but his need to show off in front of his friends and his refusal to listen to his teachers was cause for concern.

A year later, at the parent-teacher interview at his new school, Marek and I were nonplussed as the teacher described our son: 'Alex is a rules man. He knows the rules, follows them and makes sure that others do too.' We wondered if she was talking about another Alex. We told her what Alex had been like at pre-school and she did not believe us. Marek and I had frozen our perception of Alex: he was an exuberant, loud child who would pose problems for all his teachers. Now into his third year at school, he is yet to antagonise even one.

I spent months dreading the day that Alex was assigned homework. I could not imagine forcing such a strong-willed child to stop playing and discipline himself. I expected major battles ahead. Yet Alex sits down as soon as he comes home from school on Monday and completes the whole week in one sitting. (Admittedly, he is supposed to pace himself and do a little each night but I choose not to tamper with my gift.) Zac, who I always perceived as the more compliant son, generally needs me to remind him about homework several times an afternoon.

The longer I have known these two kaleidoscopic characters, the harder I find it to generalise about who they are. Having collected so much evidence both for and against any personality trait I care to consider, I have come to see each of them as vast potentialities rather than fixed identities. Life with them is unpredictable, fascinating and ever-evolving. They will continue to surprise me on a daily basis as long as I stay awake to the fact that they are walking question marks.

BOREDOM IN OUR CHILDREN

What worries me about our children's generation is how little opportunity they have to find themselves bored. For some children the reason is their tight schedule but for most it is because of all the technological options for stimulation: computers, DVDs, play-stations, Nintendos, mobile phones with games, and many more. Without the occasional spot of boredom, children have less opportunity to develop the resourcefulness to deal with it. Moreover, a small taste of boredom can be the trigger for physical activity, something children eventually lack if they always have a remote or a mouse in their hand.

I have written a memoir for a family where the children grew up on an isolated farm in the 1950s. With parents too busy to provide any entertainment for them, the four children were without neighbours, television, transport and shops. Were they ever bored? They must have been from time to time. But look where it led. When I re-open their story, I read about how they made their own toys, put on magic shows, and constructed space ships, cubby houses and model aeroplanes. They simulated their own version of the car rally that used to pass through the nearest town, using matchbox cars and designing complex networks of roads in their sandpit. They played imaginary games for hours. They put together their own family magazine full of their drawings, poetry, games, quizzes and stories. They made scrap books (including one to commemorate the long-anticipated visit of Queen Elizabeth II to Australia). They read books, comics and their set of encyclopedias. They enjoyed nature, chasing rabbits, digging holes, exploring creeks, and climbing trees. They also did their chores.

Of course, these children enjoyed the advantage of living in a family of four children close in age. Yet I could make a similar list of the kind of creative activities my two children devise. They design comics, conduct their own physical exercise programs, put on shows full of physical feats, build Lego inventions, construct obstacle courses and cubby houses, make potions (not my favourite of their activities) and play imaginary games. Alex writes many long stories and composes 'interesting' piano pieces. Zac works on his ball skills and practises gymnastics. They like to lie around listening to music and they both love doing crossword puzzles suited to their ages. I just popped my head outside the study to ask for an example of anything else they like to make. Marek answered for them. A mess.

I remember many years ago my Norwegian friend Julia decided to move with her husband and three children, for one year, from Oslo to some Greek Island. I lost contact with her after that but I remember her words before leaving: 'I'm really looking forward to some time to be bored!' At that stage in my life, boredom had always been my enemy number one, so I found her words thought-provoking. Yet boredom can be a gift in disguise propelling us into creativity. It is often the essential condition before creative impulses can arise within us. If our children are stimulated in every free moment of their day they are less likely to turn to their imagination let alone tune in to the needs of their inner world.

One of the worst aspects of all this technological entertainment is how it all compares with household chores. How can an activity like folding clothes compete with all these diversions? For Alex, the most boring part of his week is doing his folding. In my effort to raise boys capable of performing domestic chores I insist my sons fold their own clothes. While Zac has resigned himself to the duty, Alex has never stopped feeling furious about a job which feels to him so intolerably boring. For a while he tried the trick of throwing his entire pile of clean clothes into the dirty-laundry basket. When I eventually wised up and forbade such action, he tried secretly opening his window and rubbing the clean clothes on the dirty window-ledge to stop me from questioning their presence in the dirty-laundry basket.

While I eventually extracted a confession for that one, I had to ask: 'Alex, why do you hate folding your clothes so much?'

'Because it's so boring,' he answered predictably.

'But the act of folding is free of pain, a completely harmless activity,' I argued. 'Can't you see that it's your hatred of it that makes it painful for you and not the folding itself? If you just relaxed and did the job without adding negative thoughts, you wouldn't feel so resentful about it.'

His eyes glazed over about halfway through that speech. I suspect I was boring him with my choice of conversation topic.

At least I can claim with full confidence that Alex never utters the words, 'I'm bored'. He knows I will only answer, 'Good—you have heaps of folding to do.'

PRACTISING MINDFULNESS

To practise 'mindfulness' these days is not an activity limited to Buddhists, and in fact the word has become quite mainstream, part of the jargon of the corporate world as well as medical and psychotherapy circles. Inevitably, its growing use can dilute its original meaning, so it is worth considering the Pali word for 'mindfulness' from the Buddhist scriptures which is *sati*. In English this word most closely translates as 'remembering' in the sense of holding an object in mind. (When we become distracted from the present moment, it is because we 'forget' it.) Such remembering requires a conscious effort. Mindfulness is not just awareness, but conscious awareness. We are purposely aware of a chosen meditation object, whether it be the breath, our thoughts, our body, our surroundings or any other aspect of the present.

Practising mindfulness properly, or paying attention without adding our usual judgements, we cannot feel bored for this practice is the condition for calm contentedness where we want for nothing. Camilla has first-hand experience of this truth and allocates a morning every week to practising mindfulness. Routines that might bore other mothers are a source of peace for Camilla:

> One of the joys of being on retreat is not having to plan: you just check the schedule for the day and then live in the moment. It occurred to me that this is how monastics have lived through the centuries. Sometimes I indulge in a fantasy about becoming a Buddhist nun but as a mother of three that is not an option. So on my day at home I do things in the morning according to a written schedule and treat it like a mindfulness morning that a nun might enjoy in a monastery. The list is simply: wash up, hang the clothes, sweep, pay bills, attend to school notes. The schedule helps me live in the moment rather than spend all morning planning what I will do next or worrying that I should be doing something different.
>
> As a meditation, housework is very effective because it's simple. My accounting work takes so much mental effort that it is harder to bring mindfulness to it. With more physical work I find that I can really meditate doing that.

Sometimes it is hard to practise mindfulness of our household tasks. We might feel exhausted, irritable or unmotivated. To force ourselves to be mindful of a specific meditation object at such times might not be gentle towards ourselves. Sometimes we need to just label our state of being 'tired' and leave it at that. We don't battle against feeling tired but accept it without adding stories: *I shouldn't feel so tired and irritable, I should be mindful and cheerful. Why do I always feel like this? I should be more like Camilla. I really am an extreme case.* On and on we can go, spinning and adding and should-ing. Why not let go of such thoughts and simply *be with* whatever state we are experiencing, with an attitude of *allowing*?

We might choose to adopt some curiosity towards states of fatigue: what does 'tired' feel like in my body? What thoughts arise when I am tired? Do I need to believe them or can I just allow them to pass across my mind like clouds floating across the sky? Bringing the quality of mindfulness, and even acceptance, to our tiredness reduces the negativity of the experience. Sometimes we declare ourselves 'too tired to think' but this is one of the unsung benefits of tiredness: finally our mind might be free of all those noisy thoughts. At last, stillness.

Boredom is highly likely to arise during a meditation sit, especially if our sit occurs in the midst of a fast-paced lifestyle. When boredom arises during a sit, like anything that arises during this time, it is only a sign of a tendency we bring to our daily lives, which is all the more reason to study it rather than reject or battle against it. Why do we dislike it so much? What are we clinging to?

Practising Buddhist teachings will not necessarily eliminate, once and for all, the arising of any of our different mind states, such as feeling tired, anxious or angry, but it definitely changes our relationship with those mind states. We develop the ability to watch them arise yet attach to them less. We increase our tolerance of them and this affects the intensity of the experience as well as the actions we might take. Rather than being exasperated with ourselves for experiencing negative emotions, we start to become gentle, accepting and forgiving. Do this for ourselves and it becomes easier to do it for others as well.

Discovering joy

For Camilla, boredom is almost a complete stranger. She experiences states of joy in meditation which she is able to bring into each day of her life. Joy arises for her in the most 'ordinary' of circumstances.

No two meditation sittings are ever the same, so I see meditating as a travel adventure where each time I wonder what will happen. Since I enjoy my sits I'm motivated to sit regularly, and I find some pleasant mind states arise. Committed to breath awareness, but still welcoming any thoughts and feelings that arise, I have become much more aware of the breath throughout my day.

For me, the idea of reaching joyful states on a meditation cushion never really motivated me. You can do that easily with drugs or alcohol. To me, meditation was always about increasing my ability to be mindful in daily life. Just as my son who is a gymnast needs to condition his body in order to do gym, I see meditation as a conditioning process where I'm strengthening that mindfulness muscle or my ability to come back into the moment. So it has come as a surprise to me that regular bouts of joy have become part of my life as a direct result of my meditation practice.

Even when doing the housework or hanging out with the kids I can experience a shift in awareness where I am no longer so incredibly central but just part of a larger process. I become a bit player in the rhythm of life rather than the centre of the universe, and this is a far more realistic perspective.

Of course, Camilla is one of those meditators who experience a high degree of joy in a sitting. Yet everyone is on a different journey and not every meditator experiences this for there may be important obstacles to address before joy can arise. Becoming attached to the idea that we must experience joy in meditation or daily life is not helpful for we need to accept whatever arises rather than contrive an experience. Still, when we feel a subtle glimmer of joy arise within us, whatever the time of day, we can pause, open to it and feel it deeply rather than rush on to the next duty. Taking a few moments to really be with our joy when it arises is good for our karma in that, when we allow ourselves to fully experience joy, we create the conditions for it to arise more often.

It is worth asking ourselves, what might be the conditions required for joy to arise within me more frequently? Being in nature? Being kind to others? Pausing to watch our children? Consciously relaxing our muscles? Exercising? Opening fully to the present moment? Cultivating curiosity and openness? Perhaps joy arises in moments when we temporarily surrender our commitment to our to-do list, taking a break from our purpose-driven way of being. Of equal importance, what are the conditions that might stifle joy in our lives? Are we habitually too harsh on ourselves? Are we addicted to worrying? Do we never stop rushing? Do we frown all day long? Or do we forget to pay attention to those small details in our lives that might fill us with gratitude and love?

For me, a daily moment of joy arises from holding Alex's hand as we walk along the street. Admittedly, this joy is tinged with relief as for the first four years of his life he refused to hold my hand in his constant efforts to run away and explore his surroundings. Still, one day he will no longer want to hold my hand in the street, so knowing how special this experience is I always feel a surge of joy on picking him up from school, when he places his sticky little hand in mine.

A well-known spiritual teacher and author who draws heavily on Buddhist teachings, Eckhart Tolle, has a gift for expressing ancient teachings in fresh, inspiring ways. In *A New Earth*, he offers these words for buying groceries, doing our laundry or anything we find boring:

> . . . let them be a vehicle for alertness. Be absolutely present in what you do and sense the alert, alive stillness within you in the background of the activity. You will soon find that what you do in such a state of heightened awareness, instead of being stressful, tedious, or irritating, is actually becoming enjoyable. To be more precise, what you are enjoying is not really the outward action but the inner dimension of consciousness that flows into the action. This is finding the joy of Being in what you are doing. If you feel your life lacks significance or is too stressful or tedious, it is because you haven't brought that dimension into your life yet . . .
>
> Joy does not come from what you do, it flows into what you do and thus into this world from deep within you.

Inquiry

- Do you seek happiness purely from sources outside yourself? Do you recognise the importance of cultivating it within?
- Are attitudes of gratitude and appreciation a part of your every day?
- Do you have ways of teaching your children to practise gratitude?
- Have you experimented with practising conscious awareness as an antidote to boredom?
- Are you able to bring a questioning approach to your life, one where you don't seek answers but remain open to the mystery and wonder of everything you perceive?

- Can you see any of the gifts of boredom? Have you noticed how it can lead to creative and imaginative action?
- Do you *allow* yourself to feel tired, angry, anxious? Do you practise *being with* unpleasant emotions, developing acceptance of their presence?
- Is there enough joy in your life? What could you do to inject more? Could more awareness of the present moment increase your capacity to feel joy?

CHAPTER 4

explaining

RELIGION, SEX, POLITICS, VIOLENCE, drugs—mothers need to have all the answers ready to deliver in age-appropriate language. Where do you go when you die? Do you believe in God, Mum? How are babies made? Who is the boss of the country? We may feel utterly ignorant in one, or more, of these areas, but this will not save us from having to make a statement—in most cases, sooner than we were hoping. The Buddha lived 2500 years ago; could his teachings possibly help us discuss with our children modern issues such as raunch culture, designer drugs, the spiritual supermarket and various global threats? Of course, the Buddha never mentioned any of these modern phenomena by name, but he did suggest an attitude we can bring to any tricky question our children pose. Consider this quotation: 'To be attached to a certain view and to look down upon other views as inferior—this the wise men call a fetter.'

The Buddha warned repeatedly that any attachment to our personal views is a great obstacle on the path to freedom from suffering. Holding views is natural, and inevitable, but clinging to them is a problem. Quoting the Buddha again: 'It is not proper for a wise man who maintains truth to come to the conclusion: This alone is Truth, and everything else is false.'

We are attached to our views when we use them as a source of identity—adding another layer to our construction of a false sense of self—or when we use them to bolster our ego, to enhance feelings of separation from others or to fuel anger or indignation. Even the Buddha's teachings are not the Truth but the 'raft' we use to reach the other shore—on arriving, we can dispense with them.

I find the Buddha's warning against clinging to views extremely helpful as I go about answering the barrage of queries from my children. Their questions are not a signal for me to present my manifesto, or any rant I may have crafted over the years, but an opportunity for my child to make a choice and practise their decision-making skills. After all, who am I to tell my children what to think? How will they learn to think for themselves if I see them as empty vessels waiting to have all my views poured into them? Isn't doing this just treating my children as property awaiting my rubber-stamp of ownership? Besides, how can I be sure my answers are right? I will still share my values with them, but when there is a choice to make on what to believe, I allow them the autonomy to be their own person.

Practising non-attachment to views, we might for example present the full range of religious options available, from which point they make up their own minds. We explain the stance of each political party but allow our child to decide for themselves which one they might eventually vote for. During such discussions with Zac, I find he will always ask me, 'But what do *you* think, Mum?' I explain my own (hopefully loosely held) opinion but balance it by telling him Marek's opinion as well—which is often different—or some other family member's opinion. Zac gains valuable experience in weighing competing arguments and turning inward to see what he thinks for himself—and he seems to enjoy this process and feel empowered by it.

Answering the big questions is often an opportunity to share our values—such as treating others with respect and making choices that avoid harm to ourselves and others—but we need to respect our children's right to choose for themselves. Even our governments at least claim to respect the right to freedom of speech. Freedom of thought is seen as a basic right in a democracy, yet many parents expect their children to hold exactly their views, from religion through to politics. For some children, this must eventually feel like living in a police state, denied their most basic democratic rights.

Gandhi had a similar message to that of the Buddha when he said:

Truth resides in every human heart, and one has to search for it there and to be guided by the truth as one sees it. But no one has the right to coerce others to act according to his own view of truth.

Venerable Thich Nhat Hanh is specific about sparing children from our views in the third of his Fourteen Mindfulness Trainings.

Aware of the suffering brought about when we impose our views on others, we are committed not to force others, even our children, by any means whatsoever—such as authority, threat, money, propaganda, or indoctrination—to adopt our views. We will respect the right of others to be different and to choose what to believe and how to decide. We will, however, help others renounce fanaticism and narrowness through practicing deeply and engaging in compassionate dialogue.

What is fascinating is that the first three of his Mindfulness Trainings all relate to the importance of non-attachment to our views even, or *especially*, so-called Buddhist views. For a monk of his standing to so prioritise this teaching suggests that attachment to views is one attachment worth investigating deeply in our lives.

TALKING ABOUT SEX

In Chapter 1 we looked at the human tendency to 'add' to our experiences. To any experience we add, for example, our biases, dramas, fears, worries and ego needs, making our lives so much more complex than they need to be. Sex is an area in which the average adult brings all manner of personal baggage. For some of us, it can feel like such a complex, overwhelming and confusing area that we avoid discussing it with our children until the time is right, little realising that as long as we fear raising the issue, the time will never feel right.

If we see sex as a topic to endlessly postpone discussing, we might miss the opportunity to practise open communication with our children on the very topics we most need to be approachable about. Many parents justify their silence by saying they do not want their children to 'lose their innocence', but maybe there is more at stake from keeping them ignorant. Driving to pick up the children from school one day, my radio station featured the leading sex educator Dr Martha Gelin who passionately pleaded with parents to talk more with their children about sex. I found her basic message to resonate with a Zen Buddhist approach in that she advocated speaking plainly, presenting the unembellished facts, and seeing sex for what it is—just another part of life.

Feeling I may have neglected this area myself, I borrowed her book from the library, to find she mounts a compelling case. The very sexual disasters we fear happening to our children—rape, sexual exploitation, unwanted pregnancies, sexual diseases—are more likely to happen if our children are uninformed and left to do all their own research without our guidance. A parent's job, in her view, is to teach children the skills of self-protection and sexual decision-making. She reminds us that most of us aspire to running homes where we can discuss anything together, especially topics that might worry our children. We need, she argues, to become comfortable about openly referring to private parts by their correct names so that there can be a foundation language on which to build future discussion.

Dr Gelin even encourages us to actively create opportunities to discuss sex with our children, possibly drawing on media images around us if our children do not feed us the questions directly. After all, if we do not answer their questions then we leave it to their peers, the internet and the rest of the media. If we want to teach them our values—which might include mutual respect or commitment between sexual partners, the importance of safety or their freedom to say 'no'—we need to express these repeatedly, and early in their life, rather than in a one-off discussion about the birds and the bees when they turn nine.

If we want our children to learn the values that will keep them safe, then we need to cultivate an open atmosphere when it comes to talking about sex. We want to convey the message that talking about sex is no big deal, so rather than an intense face-to-face encounter, we keep it low-key and discuss sex whenever it naturally arises as a topic, whether we are driving in our cars or doing housework. As always, we use our intuition over how much detail to provide, taking into account their age and level of maturity.

In her eye-opening and often saddening book *What's Happening to Our Girls?* author Maggie Hamilton takes us a few years down the track to show what could happen—perhaps a worst–case scenario—if we neglect to discuss sex with our daughters:

> When girls don't get the chance to have important and meaningful conversations about sex with their parents, it's hard for them to be clear about boundaries they are comfortable with. They may end up doing whatever their peers expect. 'I do see a number of girls sorry they've got into sexual situations they weren't happy with,' one school counsellor told me. 'Often these girls are desperate to be accepted. Boys say, "You've got to give us head to be accepted", so they do and are shunned.' This was a frequent story. A number of teachers and counsellors spoke to me of the 'Monday morning syndrome', where girls arrive at school totally devastated by an experience, generally sexual, they had when out with their peers over the weekend.

Maggie emphasises throughout her book that the world these children inhabit is radically different from the one their parents can remember, with completely new issues and values to navigate. Our children need good information and parents who understand something of the culture surrounding their daughters. We all need to become clear, calm straight-talkers when it comes to discussing sex with our children.

WEB ENCOUNTERS

It was a week night. Marek would be out at a seminar and I wanted to attend the weekly meeting of my Buddhist group. There would be one hour where the children needed a babysitter and at short notice the pickings were slim. I did not have much faith in the skills of the only babysitter available, but it would only be an hour—what could go wrong? When I left the babysitter, who was already lying down on the couch to read the newspaper, Zac was watching TV and Alex was playing computer games.

I arrived home around ten o'clock to discover that rather a lot had gone wrong. Marek had been delayed so the babysitter was at our house for four hours instead of only one and had not moved from the couch the entire time. The boys had only just gone to bed with Marek's assistance, and I felt angry and agitated that they had sat in front of screens for all that time. My need for the house to be under control in my absence had been flouted.

By 10.30, I was just about to turn the light off and go to sleep when Marek remarked, 'I think Alex might have visited some questionable websites. He asked me if licking a penis is part of sex.'

'What!' I shrieked, rising to sit bolt upright. I ran to the study and switched on the computer to view the recent history of sites visited. My five-year-old son, it appeared, had typed 'sex' into Google. Clicking the various links offered he had visited around ten different sites. Fortunately, our filters are such that he did not see anything too sick or violent, but he certainly witnessed a great deal of the modern smorgasbord of internet porn.

I panicked. I knew of no other five year olds in the whole world who had seen such images. Just mine. I had failed to protect my son. His innocence was destroyed forever. How could I have let this happen? Fear kicked in as I could see him talking about the sites at school the next day to his friends in kindergarten. This was a full-blown disaster. I had to talk to him. But what would I say?

I stayed on the computer until midnight surfing the net for advice. Most of the sites offering advice on my quandary were run by religious extremists, people likely to be attached to their views. A common theme in the advice I read on the more moderate sites, however, was that I should avoid reacting with panic in front of Alex as that might make me unapproachable when issues arose in the future. Rather, I needed to calmly request that he avoid such sites in the future and talk to me if he has any questions.

The next morning, before school, I followed this advice and explained sex to him in the plainest and simplest of terms, emphasising that the best place for it is in a loving relationship between grown-ups, before impressing on him the importance of keeping his mouth shut at school about his new discoveries.

My feelings of remorse took a day or two to fade away and I did not use any babysitters for the next few months. Yet with the passage of time Alex remains, to all appearances, unaffected by the experience and these days I even wonder what I was so upset about.

In *Why TV is Good for Kids*, a book that attempts to douse myriad moral panics fuelled by the media, authors Lumby and Fine report there is no evidence to support the widely held view that the slightest contact with pornography will have lasting toxic effects on children. They assure us that children who spend any time online will come across pornography and that this is likely to happen well before their parents are aware of it.

An issue conducive to knee-jerk, hysterical reactions—if we take my own as an example—Lumby and Fine also discuss the tendency of conservative commentators to 'talk about sexually explicit material as if it was all the same', as though the evils of child pornography could possibly be in the same category as the more common versions of pornography. Lumby and Fine join other moderate voices on this topic in asking parents not to avoid the topic: 'The last thing you want is a child who is too scared to tell you that something has distressed them in case they get blamed for looking at it.'

When it comes to these dreaded web encounters, a Buddhist approach can help: don't panic, speak calmly and keep some perspective.

Maggie Hamilton provides helpful advice on what to say to our children about pornography and I believe her suggestions are equally relevant to boys. While this is not what I would say to Alex at five years old after only one experience, we can tweak this message to suit the age and gender of our children.

> It is important parents explain that in porn, sex is often violent and uncaring, and that many of the girls in porn films do so because they have been sexually abused, live on the streets or have a drug habit, and that these films perpetuate their abuse. It helps for parents to remind girls that good sex is about caring and not treating a person like an object. Girls also need to know that people who get hooked on porn find it hard to express the warm and nurturing feelings that make relationships special.

TALKING ABOUT DEATH

One day, Zac threw a coin into a well and made a wish. A few days later, I started wondering what his wish was so, at the risk of prying, I asked him. His answer: 'That nobody will die ever again.' Hmmm, I thought, here was one wish that would never come true.

The certainty of death does not sit comfortably with children—nor their parents. How we handle the subject will depend on whether the context is one of curiosity from our child or the highly emotional atmosphere following the death of someone they love. As with most issues, however, we need to portray ourselves to our children as open to discussion, so that communication on any issue that disturbs them is always an option.

The average mother feels at more of a loss explaining death than she does explaining any of the other big questions. How can we comfort our children, for example, if our own fears and questions about death are unresolved? Not so long ago death was around every corner, but in modern times, most of us lack experience in coping with death. Death of babies and young children, for most of human history, has been commonplace. Life expectancies were shorter and, without the advantages of modern medicine, more adults died in the prime of their lives.

As we can well imagine, the Buddha heard many questions about death. One woman, named Kisa Gotami, was mad with grief at the death of her baby son. Refusing to accept his death, she approached house after house in her town asking for medicine to cure him. Finally a friend suggested she approach the Buddha. The Buddha told her to go into town and fetch a mustard seed, but he prescribed that the seed had to come from a house where nobody had ever died.

Kisa Gotami again went from house to house, but everyone had the same story: *My husband died last year; My daughter died three years ago; My brother died here yesterday.* She had her baby son cremated and returned to the Buddha empty-handed, telling him, 'I'm not the only one who has lost a loved one. Everywhere people have died. All things pass away.' Kisa Gotami was ordained as a nun and, assisted by her insight into impermanence, soon became awakened, or free from suffering.

Ours is a culture where death is treated as the exception, not the rule. We live as though it will never happen, and avoid thinking or talking about it. Yet children want to address death. If we ignore their questions, we teach them it is best to suppress our pain and suffering, even though these are an integral part of our lives. Some of our reluctance to talk about death with our children surely comes from the fact that we don't know what happens after we die. We are not comfortable with uncertainty, with not-knowing, and prefer to address topics with pat answers.

When my sons have asked me where we go when we die, I have told them about how some people believe in reincarnation, others in heaven and hell. Some believe there is no afterlife, that death is the end, and others believe that the dead are here with us or that they live on in our hearts and memories. I tell them they can make up their own minds what to believe or they can join the millions who choose to surrender to the mystery. None of these answers can be particularly satisfying for them, but that is our lot as human beings. When they ask, 'But what do you think, Mum?' I tell them that I do not know. It helps if you have a parenting philosophy that allows you to lack answers from time to time. They might even think, *Mum is okay about not knowing everything so maybe I can be too.*

I realise Buddhists, especially in the Tibetan tradition, have a reputation for believing in reincarnation. Yet the Buddhists I mix with in my tradition, called Insight (a Western, non-monastic version of Theravada), rarely even talk about rebirth, let alone 'believe' in it. In my Buddhist circles, the teachers constantly emphasise that the Buddha taught a practice: he gave us things to *do* rather than propositions to *believe* in. In the book *Buddhism Without Beliefs* Stephen Batchelor explains: 'The Buddha was not a mystic . . . He did not claim to have had an experience that granted him privileged, esoteric knowledge of how the universe ticks.'

The Buddha taught that becoming overly concerned about what happens after you die was a potential time-waster. Why speculate about an unknowable future? Our problem, right here and now, is suffering and dissatisfaction, and this is what the Buddha teaches us to resolve.

In the 'Parable of the Poisoned Arrow', a monk presses the Buddha for an answer about death, threatening to abandon his training if the Buddha does not satisfy him. The Buddha replies:

> It is as if a man had been wounded by a poisoned arrow and when the doctor arrives says, 'I will not allow you to remove this arrow until I have learned the caste, the age, the occupation, the birthplace, and the motivation of the person who wounded me.' That man would die before learning all this. Whatever happens after death, you are still faced with birth, old age, sorrow, grief and despair, for which I'm now prescribing the antidote.

As the Buddha said on other occasions: 'I teach suffering and the end of suffering.' He was not interested in exploring metaphysical propositions. When it comes to talking about death with our children, we need to address the issue and our feelings without becoming stuck for too long in our conjecturing. For Buddhists, it is the certainty that we will die that we need to focus on for this is what makes each moment of our life precious and meaningful.

Zac and I recently won some tickets to an opera called *The Makropulos Secret* about a woman who, after drinking an elixir, lives for hundreds of years. Despite leading the high life of a famous and widely adored singer, the woman could find no satisfaction from her life: without the prospect of death, her life felt endless and, as such, devoid of all meaning.

In cases where a child has lost someone close to them, the consensus among the experts is that 'denial' is not the answer, such as when we explain that Grandma is 'having a long sleep', or 'went away'. The Buddhanet website, an extensive site describing itself as a worldwide information and education network, offers this advice for explaining death to children:

Regardless of how strong or comforting religious beliefs may be, death means the loss of a living being, the absence of a physical presence. It is a time of sadness and mourning. It is important to help children accept the realities of death—the loss and the grief. Attempts to protect children deny them opportunities to share their feelings and receive needed support. Sharing feelings helps. Sharing religious beliefs also helps if done with sensitivity to how children perceive and understand what is happening and what is being said. It is important to check with them to find out how they are hearing and seeing events around them.

Recently, our family optometrist, Leonard, passed away at the age of sixty-six. Alex wears high-prescription glasses, so we had visited him many times over the years. No believer in 'professional distance', Leonard was always full of fun—magic tricks, jokes and warmth—beaming 'Hello, Sport!' whenever he saw Alex. The boys were shocked at the news, but being children, fully capable of moving on after a couple of minutes. All the same, that night I arranged for the three of us to conduct a small ceremony in the boy's bedroom. Sitting on cushions, we all lit a candle for Leonard and dedicated a minute of silence to him. Then we talked about his good qualities and our gratitude for the ways he had helped us. I like to think that for the boys it was a lesson in appreciating others as well as a model of a spiritual ritual which might help them to cope with death in the future.

TALKING ABOUT RELIGION

When talking about religion with Zac and Alex I have emphasised our 'family value' of critical inquiry: keeping our minds open and questioning, exploring any doubts and ultimately listening to our own inner voices. (Polish Marek has a special gift for critical thinking, having grown up in a country run on communist propaganda . . .) The Buddha has always impressed the world's free thinkers with the oft-quoted Kalama Sutta, his words to the townspeople known as the Kalamans. In this version from Nanamoli Thera's *The Life of the Buddha*, the townspeople asked the Buddha which of the many touring spiritual teachers, whose messages were often conflicting, they should believe. The Buddha famously replied:

> Do not be satisfied with hearsay or with tradition or with legendary lore or with what has come down in scriptures or with conjecture or with logical inference or with weighing evidence or with liking for a view after pondering over it or with someone else's ability or with the thought 'The monk is our teacher'. When you know in yourselves: 'These things are wholesome, blameless, commended by the wise, and being adopted and put into effect they lead to welfare and happiness,' then you should practice and abide in them.

The key words are 'know in yourselves'. Humans through the ages have been a little too comfortable with silencing their consciences, misgivings and intuition in the face of an authority figure—or the group who thinks with one mind. We have a long history of using quotations from the scriptures to justify all kinds of harmful actions. Even the less impressionable believe anything deemed 'logical' or the product of rigorous thought processes. The Buddha suggests an alternative: to know in ourselves what leads to harm and what leads to happiness, and to draw on our own direct experience, our inner wisdom. (On many occasions, this includes the wisdom to say, 'I don't know'.)

A negative side effect to overvaluing, or attaching to, this teaching of refusing to accept what we are told is that we might lose respect for people who believe in scriptures, who obey clergymen, who unthinkingly uphold traditions. One might find oneself feeling superior to those who one perceives to have switched off their own capacity to decide. Yet this would only demonstrate an attachment to a Buddhist teaching—something the Buddha warned us against. I am quite possibly guilty of such an attachment, otherwise known as religious intolerance.

I would expect someone like Miriam Stoppard, a medical specialist and prolific author of family titles, to share my value of 'critical inquiry'—and she probably does—but in her book *Questions Children Ask and How to Answer Them* I felt surprised and challenged to read about a value I had definitely overlooked in talking to my children about religion. She sees questions about religion as a chance to develop in our children the value of tolerance:

> Try to teach comparative religion. Even if you yourself have a strong religious faith and you do not agree with the beliefs of a different religion, you can still acknowledge the right of others to worship as they wish, and point out that different religions should not be in competition with one another.

Among the aspects of religion we present to our children, she starts with this suggestion for what to tell them:

> Everyone should be free to follow a religion and worship God without being troubled, because it's a private matter for you alone to decide. You can still be a good person without believing in God at all, or belonging to any particular religion. You can decide

later when you've had time to think about it. We'll still love you, whatever you decide.

Stoppard writes that a healthy spiritual life is something all children can benefit from, but she does encourage parents to allow children to make their own choices rather than forcing them to share their beliefs. Still, for her a priority seems to be that we all respect each other's choices. I have to admit that she happens to be in good company. The Venerable Thich Nhat Hanh lives to promote world peace and in his book *Living Buddha, Living Christ* writes:

> We human beings can be nourished by the best values of many traditions . . . It was only later, through friendships with Christian men and women who truly embody the spirit of understanding and compassion of Jesus, that I have been able to touch the depths of Christianity. The moment I met Martin Luther King, Jr., I knew I was in the presence of a holy person . . . And others less well known, have made me feel that Lord Jesus is still here with us.

Religious fundamentalists tend to be dogmatic, intolerant and bigoted. While Buddhism is not, strictly speaking, a religion, an overly orthodox approach to Buddhist practice might render some Buddhists no exception. Neither are many atheists and sceptics, who often exhibit a sense of intellectual superiority and can, in many cases, be the most intolerant of all.

I found myself momentarily looking down on a mother who chirped that the reason for the sunny weather for her son's party was that she had prayed for it. I have a problem with her view of such an interventionist God (surely God hears a few more desperate prayers he could attend to?), yet I also have to admit that this mother is warm and kind, and for this deserves my respect regardless of her beliefs. After all, only with religious tolerance can there be any hope of peace in our world. Only with religious tolerance will we admit that all religions have at their heart humanitarian ideals and the aim of universal well-being.

I am conscious that the notion of religious tolerance can sound very politically correct and possibly even a little unrealistic. After all, we have all met religious people whose stance is impossible to take seriously: the Christian who believes their loving God could send his children to hell for eternity, the Buddhist who thinks abused children are receiving their 'karma' for misdeeds in a past life, the atheist who feels contemptuous of any seeker.

Every belief system however gives rise to approaches which are uninformed and ridiculous—not to mention sexist. Yet within all of them are those who are deep-thinking, compassionate and inspiring. (Interestingly, the troublemakers often appear to be among those at the top of the various religious hierarchies, but don't get me started…) We can encourage our children to practise tolerance, to make their own choices but when it comes to religion, to always keep a strong connection to their own inner wisdom.

Through his own exploration Zac has experimented over the years with calling himself an atheist, a Baha'i, a Catholic, a Jews for Jesus, but these days he prefers not to label himself. Still, he loves to end his day with a Buddhist meditation which I will describe in Chapter 6.

TALKING ABOUT DRUGS AND ALCOHOL

Back in 2007, the Australian Government sent every household a magazine sealed in plastic, called *Talking with Your Kids about Drugs*.

Jaded, cynical voter that I am, I saw it as a last-ditch attempt of a floundering government to look caring. All the same, I held onto it, let it gather some dust, and a year down the track, with a new government in charge, I finally opened it—ten minutes ago. I decided to be open-minded since the public servants who conducted the research and put the document together probably do care about the issues. Still, then Prime Minister John Howard had the privilege of announcing their findings in his opening message:

> A national survey found that 93 per cent of 15 to 17 year olds were willing to talk to their parents about drugs and 92 per cent said that parents could influence them not to use drugs.

Cynicism aside, even if these figures are half true, the role of parents in stopping their children from dangerous experimentation with drugs is clearly paramount. Although our own children may not yet be teenagers, a further tip appeared a few pages on:

> Once you've had a discussion, it's important to have another. Ensure that you are always willing to speak to your children about drugs and start early.

The magazine reported the facts on each fashionable drug for parents to learn and discuss with their children but also gave some general advice with a view to prevention, some of which even chimes with a Buddhist approach. For example, the magazine exhorts us during any discussion of drugs to always remain calm and never overreact, this being the best way to keep the dialogue open.

Call me naive and unworldly but it always surprises me when I read in newspaper articles that most illegal drug taking—even in the case of heroin—involves ordinary, otherwise law-abiding citizens who regularly consume illegal drugs, enjoy it and do not become addicted. This is hardly information we would voluntarily provide to our children but it does suggest that, if we want to be parents who 'remain calm and never overreact', we need to keep our language moderate. If our words are too alarmist—*try drugs even once and you will be addicted for life, become sick, homeless and die*—we are misrepresenting the risk and damaging our credibility. While we can discuss all these risks, it would be incorrect to claim they apply to everyone who has ever tried drugs.

In our daily interactions with our children, the government's magazine suggests, we practise listening to them, avoiding conflict and setting clear boundaries. While there is nothing groundbreaking in that advice, they did highlight this message:

> One of the most effective deterrents to drug use amongst young people is a parent who is devoted to spending time with them. Someone who talks with them about their friends, what goes on at school, the sport they play, what interests them.

Again, no surprises: paying close attention and being present for our children at every stage in their development is unbeatable insurance.

The Buddha did not leave his lay followers with lists of rules to live by but he did specify five precepts which make sound general guidelines for anyone serious about practice. For example, it is difficult to practise Buddhist teachings when you are intoxicated, hence one of the precepts, along with abstaining from killing and stealing, is to abstain from intoxicants. It is up to us how far we wish to take this advice, and we come to a decision based on our own observations of our direct experience. Observing the effects of alcohol on my own mind and body, I personally avoid anything more than a glass. Needless to say, the magazine did mention the parent being an 'important role model'—so perhaps we all have added incentives to consider the Buddha's fifth precept carefully.

TALKING ABOUT CRIME AND VIOLENCE

Despite our best efforts to protect them, our children will hear some of the disturbing news of the day about terrorism, crime and war. Man's inhumanity to man is potentially a topic that could fill us with hatred and rage. That someone could hurt a child, a pregnant woman, a whole community, is beyond our understanding. So begins our dissent into what Buddhists call dualistic thinking: there are two types of people in the world, the good and the evil. Yet it is worth pondering the words of Nobel Prize-winning Russian, the late Aleksandr Solzhenitsyn, in his classic memoir *The Gulag Archipelago*:

> Gradually it was disclosed to me that the line separating good and evil passes not through states, nor between classes, nor between political parties either, but right through every human heart, and through all human hearts. This line shifts. Inside us, it oscillates with the years. Even within hearts overwhelmed by evil, one small bridgehead of good is retained; and even in the best of all hearts, there remains a small corner of evil.

Solzhenitsyn's understanding resembles the Buddhist perspective of the human condition, although Buddhists use the word 'delusion' instead of 'evil'. People commit crimes not because they are inherently bad but because of the causes and conditions at play in their lives—not least, their ignorance about the nature of reality. Criminals are likely to have suffered childhoods marked by tragic neglect and abuse. We feel so sorry for such suffering children, yet when they grow up to be criminals we want them punished harshly. The overwhelming majority of crime these days is drug related, and why do people take drugs if not to numb the pain of being alive in what, in most of their cases, is a loveless world?

What a valuable lesson for our children if we can teach them to feel compassion even for those most difficult to love. If they can manage this, how much easier it will be to practise tolerance for the various characters in the school playground. On the topic of violence, I challenge Zac and Alex to *hate the crime but love the criminal*. I challenge them to acknowledge the criminal's basic humanity and the fact that, like us, they only want to be happy, even if they are severely misguided about how to achieve this objective.

I remind the boys that if they did not have parents who loved them, parents who were sober, drug-free and capable of meeting their needs for food and shelter, they too would find it difficult to function as a perfectly normal adult. This is not to say that dangerous criminals should walk free or that they should not be held responsible for their actions, but hating them only hurts ourselves by denying ourselves the chance to own a completely loving heart.

The Buddha taught us, 'Hatred can never cease by hatred. Hatred can only cease by love'. Rather than teach our children to hate the so-called evil of the world, let's teach them the wisdom of those who consider causes and conditions. Or, to quote the nineteenth-century poet Henry Wadsworth Longfellow: 'If we could read the secret history of our enemies, we should find in each man's life sorrow and suffering enough to disarm all hostility.'

There is no better model of this lesson than the Venerable Thich Nhat Hanh who does not hesitate to use an extreme example in his book *Being Peace*:

One day we received a letter telling us about a young girl on a small boat who was raped by a Thai pirate. She was only twelve, and she jumped into the ocean and drowned herself. When you first learn of something like that, you get angry at the pirate. You naturally take the side of the girl. As you look more deeply you will see it differently. If you take the side of the little girl, then it is easy. You only have to take a gun and shoot the pirate. But we cannot do that. In my meditation I saw that if I had been born in the village of the pirate and raised in the same conditions as he was, there is a great likelihood that I would become a pirate . . .

His insight led him to write his famous poem 'Call Me By My True Names'. Here is an excerpt:

I am the frog swimming happily in the clear pond,
and I am also the grass-snake who, approaching in silence,
feeds itself on the frog.

I am the child in Uganda, all skin and bones,
my legs as thin as bamboo sticks,
and I am the arms merchant, selling deadly weapons to
    Uganda.

I am the twelve-year-old girl, refugee on a small boat,
who throws herself into the ocean after being raped by a sea
    pirate,
and I am the pirate, my heart not yet capable of seeing and
    loving.

Zac and I have been reading aloud together *The Boy in the Striped Pyjamas*, the story of a German nine-year-old boy whose father is appointed the Commandant of the Auschwitz concentration camp. In his effort to understand the story Zac tries to divide the characters into those who are 'good' and 'bad'. Interestingly, most of the characters are, as in real life, a complex mixture of strengths and weaknesses. Even in the case of the characters who commit inexcusable atrocities, there are always causes and conditions—be they cultural, historical, genetic or otherwise. The causes for the rise of Nazism are beyond the scope of this book but suffice it to say that the treaty of Versailles signed at the end of the First World War inflicted such harsh penalties on Germans that they suffered poverty and humiliation, thus sowing many of the seeds of Nazism.

•

When it comes to explaining the world to our children, we could factor in the advice of mother, author and psychotherapist Stephanie Dowrick who believes parents could talk a lot less:

> I hear people overloading their children with long explanations that veer between the confusing and the boring. 'Talk less and listen more' works for all relationships; children are no exception. Often our over-talking is a symptom of our own anxiety; it adds to theirs. If they want more information, they'll ask for it.

Inquiry

- Do you allow your children to arrive at their own views, respecting their autonomy?
- Is sex a topic that you can discuss openly with your children or do you postpone it?

- How would you respond to your child viewing internet pornography? Could you approach the situation calmly in order to keep the communication between you open?
- Do you allow your children opportunities to discuss their feelings about death? Can you discuss it openly with them?
- When talking with your children about religion, do you teach the values of both critical questioning as well as tolerance and respect for differing beliefs?
- Are you aware of the value in continuing to pay close attention to your child, taking an interest in the details of their life, if you want them to avoid drug abuse?
- Do you teach your children that criminals are evil scum or that their behaviour is only the result of the causes and conditions at play in their lives?

CHAPTER 5

socialising

As we make new friends among the mothers at school, some of us notice amusing parallels with our days of courtship, our 'dating' years. Many of us, for example, in our efforts to recruit allies have developed mental checklists resembling those we used for finding our life partner. Our checklists help us assess compatibility: similar parenting philosophy—tick; good sense of humour—tick; wide conversational range—tick; capable of listening to me—tick. In another parallel to the world of dating, we find ourselves dealing with the consequences of the inevitable misjudgements: some will need to 'dump', or come to terms with being 'dumped'—always heart-wrenching whatever side we are on. And who has not witnessed, if not participated in, that delicate situation where Susan introduces two friends only to find they have more in common with each other than they ever did with her?

Close friendships take time and many mothers talk of a pragmatic need to limit the number of friends they engage with. Issues arising from finding a balance between too many friends, or too few, can demand considerable mental space. Close relationships with other mothers can become fraught, for these days we might require not only compatibility with the other mother but also between our children and husbands. What do we do, for example, if our child refuses to see their friend, perhaps understandably, even though each of the parents still enjoy their friendship? Such are the moral dilemmas we navigate.

All kinds of social scenarios await a mother when her children start school. For the most fortunate among us, starting school feels like a glorious reunion with all the parents we have met over the past few years. Others find themselves gazing onto long-established clique groups wondering if they have the energy to infiltrate one. Mothers with children born three years apart find they have missed valuable social history shared by mothers with children born two years apart.

Mothers of boys might gravitate to each other, as might mothers of girls. Many are disturbed to find their friendships dictated more by convenience than compatibility.

While some mothers are content with their social situation at school, others feel alienated, as they seem to fit in nowhere. Work commitments may have cut into time to mix with other parents. In some cases our children might be struggling socially, which tends to reduce our own opportunities to meet other parents. Some mothers feel they have little in common with the mothers at school, and more mothers than we realise may appear socially withdrawn as one of the symptoms of a battle with depression. Mothers who join a school mid-term often feel insufficiently welcomed, if not invisible, around mothers whose friendships have long settled.

While mothers who are not all that emotionally involved with inter-parent relationships do exist, there are probably more who have hopes, fears and expectations concerning other parents. While the odd mother may feel sufficiently engaged with alternative social groups to not need a sense of belonging at school, it would be more common in the early school years for mothers to yearn for a sense of social connection and community.

With such a potential diversity of social experiences, there are plenty of reasons to approach all the members of our school community with compassion. Who knows what is the inner experience for each parent we see in the school playground at pick-up time? We can give her an automatic smile, as part of the routine, so she does not think we are unfriendly. Or we could practise presence in the moment, to ensure our smile comes from a space of unconditional compassion and loving-kindness. After all, relationships with other parents provide one more opportunity to practise our deepest values and the virtues most of us aspire to: patience, forgiveness, tolerance and generosity.

EVERYONE IS IN NEED

Sydney Buddhist teacher Subhana Barzaghi decided to take a group
of Buddhists on an excursion to a shopping mall. She instructed each
person to select their favourite type of shop and the group visited
each of these in turn. The aim of the exercise was to be mindful of
the arising of craving for certain objects, yet *not buy anything*. The
group found themselves in a shoe shop for one man, a professor with
a taste for Italian shoes, a lingerie shop for one of the women and a
baby clothes shop for another woman about to adopt a child. Yet as
Zen Buddhists, who often come from intellectual backgrounds, most
of them chose the bookshop.

One of the women approached Subhana and begged to be able to
buy the book she had found. If Subhana did not agree, she explained,
she would have to drive all the way back the following day, and this
would be very inconvenient. Subhana, of course, allowed her to buy
the book, and afterwards they all reconvened to discuss the excursion.
Faced with each of their desires for the various objects of consumption,
Subhana asked them to contemplate the question, 'What was it I really
wanted?' At first their answers were about opportunities to look good,
feel good, or enjoy the object and what it offered.

Yet as Subhana continued asking, 'But why do you want that?
Why do you want to look good/feel good/enjoy that object,' all
the answers started to sound the same: everybody was looking for
connection with other human beings and, at some level, hoped that
the shoes, lingerie, baby clothes or books would help them find that
increased intimacy. In the case of those who wanted non-fiction books,
group members believed that others would respect them more if they
bore such knowledge. Others wanted to read similar authors to their
friends, to share an experience. They all wanted to enjoy a sense of

connection with the author, or the characters, or to learn more about what the human experience is like for others.

The professor in the group wanted to buy a book to help him with his research so that he could be published. A year later, he called Subhana from interstate to tell her that he was now published but realised that had not been what he really wanted after all. A published book turned out merely to be his perception of what it would take to achieve meaningful connections with others.

On hearing about Subhana's excursion, I felt instantly defensive. I love reading and devour books and newspaper articles for sheer enjoyment, surely not due to any social neediness. Then I considered how I have always sought the company of engaging characters between the pages of books, how I have favoured readers as friends so we can talk about books. I have peppered so many of my conversations with charming quotations or interesting facts gleaned from books and newspapers. For the intimacy of sharing a literary experience with friends, I have read whatever they recommended. I have quoted the views of newspaper columnists so that the well-informed would approve of me. I have tried to read something interesting before a dinner party. I have lapped up biographies for insights into the human condition that might shed meaning on the lives of those I live with and on mine. So yes, we do read and partake in many other activities—travel, work, music, sport, art—largely out of a need for meaningful connection with others.

The way we use the internet has provided further proof—which nobody expected—of the depth of our need to engage meaningfully with others. Many expected the explosion in the availability of information to increase our cultural diversity, but the opposite has happened. When it comes to sales of DVDs, music and books, for example, people have purchased more of fewer and fewer titles. Not only that, most of us tend to frequent a narrow selection of the total number of websites available. Despite an abundance of choices, we all converge on the most popular selections. Anita Elberse, an associate professor at Harvard Business School who has studied these trends, describes one of the main reasons: 'People are inherently social, and therefore find value in listening to the same music and watching the same movies that others do.'

Given these universal social needs, to what extent do each of us feel we achieve meaningful connection with others? One secret that many mothers may harbour is their loneliness. Sonia, a mother of three, expresses what many of us may feel from time to time:

I am a relatively independent, self-reliant person, yet I am struck by how lonely adult life can often feel. I do have friends, old and new, yet everyone is so busy that it can be a long time between meetings. When you don't see people so often, the quality of the connection suffers and you don't end up sharing so much about yourself. It takes a lot of work to keep in contact with close friends and many women give up the effort.

Sometimes I notice, Gee, it's been several days since I've had a conversation longer than one minute with another adult! Sometimes I'm really in the mood for some company yet the chances of another adult being free at that exact moment are so slim it is hardly worth trying to contact anyone. Friendship is strictly by appointment or fluke meetings. Even my husband and I can go several days between conversations. I have accepted that this is the way it is, but it is interesting that nobody speaks about the loneliness of adulthood.

If we feel despondent about our isolation we are also likely to tell ourselves that we are the only person who feels this way, especially if we live on the outer fringes of a thriving clique group. We see everybody around us as blissfully connected, and fail to recognise that when it comes to human relations, everyone nurses strong needs, longings and sensitivities.

Unlike the early years of motherhood when we all had similar sorts of problems—sleep, feeding, crying, career disruption—these days there is a great diversity of struggles for mothers so they are more likely to feel alone with their worries. If a mother has problems with her school-aged child it could be about any one of a vast range of issues: learning difficulties, a dislike of school, a poor relationship with the teacher, or a struggle to perform in any number of areas, be it the classroom, the playground or the sports field. It becomes harder for mothers to find women grappling with the same issues. In fact, it is hardly uncommon for a mother to be socially ostracised as a result of her child's problems.

THE NEED TO BE SEEN

Every mother has a need to connect, a need to belong, but also, interestingly, a need to be seen. The Buddha spoke of our craving to 'be', which translates into any social context as a need to be seen, for others to confirm our existence. We have a craving *to be seen* and, in most cases, we not only want our existence to be confirmed but also validated or met with approval.

I remember when Alex was still at pre-school, one mother there was widely resented and criticised: her crime was simply being lax with her greetings of other parents. She would stare straight through them, or only acknowledge them in a cursory way that left them feeling unseen, invisible and a little insulted. I had the opportunity to talk to this mother at length alongside sports fields where older siblings played cricket, so I learned that, as a mother of three, she found the school-run highly stressful and that her unfortunate demeanour did not spring from any ill-will towards other parents. Yet her failure to acknowledge this need to be seen in the other parents made her a figure of contempt.

What interested me about this scenario is the strength of our craving to be seen and how angry we can feel if it is not honoured. When we say, 'Hi, how are you—I like your jumper!', on another level we are saying, 'I see you, you are not invisible,' and the recipient feels relieved to have their craving to be seen fulfilled. We might dismiss such banter as small talk but it is a vital ingredient in any social setting. To have our presence acknowledged, our opinion heard, our name remembered and used, is all part of this desire. It is the reason we sometimes make seemingly inane remarks such as, 'I saw you yesterday on the corner of Archer and Gibbs Street.' Again, we are recognising the common human craving to be seen, in order to confirm that we exist.

A psychologist by trade, Subhana points out that our need to be seen and heard is at its strongest in childhood. In her words:

Attunement and connection in early childhood development is essential and is how the child learns emotional regulation and develops a healthy self-esteem. Yet how many missed opportunities there are, when we don't pay attention and mindfully connect, due to our busyness as parents.

I attended a retreat with a pioneering Buddhist teacher, Gregory Kramer, from the United States who speaks regularly about this craving to be seen. With his unconventional approach to Buddhist practice, he emphasises the importance of interpersonal relationships. On his retreats, most of the meditation happens in pairs or groups, where retreatants engage in dialogues on given topics, paying close attention to each other, listening deeply, allowing pauses and practising openness. His retreats provide a fascinating learning experience, but occasionally I felt painfully self-conscious sitting face to face with a new person and I noticed a craving to *not* be seen.

Sometimes we want to sink into the background, unnoticed, savouring privacy and anonymity. Or we cannot bring ourselves to look into the eyes of another in case they see the real 'me'. As the Buddha taught, another craving is to 'not be', or the craving for non-existence.

This is the craving for oblivion and, in its extreme forms, manifests as various attempts at escape such as alcoholism, drug abuse or suicide. In a social context, this craving to 'not be' translates as a craving to 'not be seen'. As with all desires, these two, to be seen or not seen, are often conflicting and confusing, yet watching their back-and-forth dance is potentially eye-opening. We might find ourselves wondering: 'I want to be friends with the parents at school (I need to be seen), yet today I don't feel like talking to anyone (I need to be not seen).'

Often, all we are aware of is how secure and comfortable, or not, we ourselves feel socially. Walking into a gathering of parents, feeling shy in those initial moments, we can feel so very centre-of-the-universe: our craving for security blinds us to the needs of others. Most people take refuge in alcohol, if it is available. Yet to remember that everyone else at a gathering has such similar needs to my own, and to actively seek to put others at ease, rather than only myself, is a brilliant escape from the prison of self-absorption.

Stephanie Dowrick, prolific author of inspirational books, wrote in one of her newspaper columns about how we routinely underestimate our own personal power in a social context and overestimate that of other people:

I am amazed at how many people complain about feeling left out or overlooked while never considering how they might save others from similar experiences . . . Some people are naturally attuned to others, always keeping an eye out for those on the margins or those feeling new or unsure in any social situation. They are society's treasures and we can all learn from them.

Dilemmas galore

One social dilemma that will challenge nearly every mother is that of differing boundaries. One mother wants a close relationship between families while another wants more space. This is a particular issue between next-door neighbours: how much time can members of one family spend with another before imposing? I have been surprised, in my own local area, at the number of next-door neighbouring mothers who no longer speak to each other due to mismatched expectations. Yet it is not only next-door neighbours, as most of us know too well. Sandra has a boundary issue with a mother living around the corner:

My latest social dilemma comes from feeling smothered. A friend has children the same age as mine and seems to constantly want to marry the two families. For her, family life runs more smoothly when she is with us, but for us it is the opposite. Being school holidays, the problem is really coming to a head for me with her constant phone calls. She doesn't understand our need for the occasional quiet day at home to ourselves. Although I often say no to her suggestions, she does not pick up the message that we need more space. Even my children are growing tired of being with them.

I'm in such a difficult position because I can empathise with her loneliness and I can see how she suffers from her assumption that she must keep her children constantly busy. Yet my family needs more quiet time—as well as time to see other different friends.

Of course, it is also painful to be on the other side of this dilemma and discover that a mother we deemed a close friend, whose company we enjoyed, needs to see a lot less of us. Yet this is only the beginning of a long list of dilemmas mothers may confront. What do we do when our friends' children are unkind, rough or a bad influence on our own? What if a friend has conflicting standards about screen time, junk food or levels of supervision? What if there is a personality clash between members of one family and another? How do we react when we realise that a so-called friend does not want the best for us but is in fact busily competing with us? It is little wonder that many mothers retreat into insularity, perhaps agreeing with philosopher Jean-Paul Sartre, who said, '*L'enfer, c'est les autres*'—hell is other people.

Even the best of friendships need to weather numerous shifts, changes and challenges, for no family is standing still. Everybody is dealing with the inevitability of change, upheaval and growth. Any 'honeymoon' period, to return to the courtship metaphor, will fade somewhat, if not end. The challenge of a Buddhist approach to all the dilemmas, to all the flux, is to cultivate equanimity—that ability to remain calm and ungrasping through highs and lows alike.

Through the shocks, betrayals and disappointments, as much as through the intimacy, support and mutual appreciation, we can strive to maintain a sense of spaciousness and perspective. This means never allowing relationship dilemmas to consume too much of our thinking. Pettiness, in particular, is a Buddhist's enemy *numero uno*. Not that we suppress pettiness if it arises; rather, we observe and understand how it undermines our equanimity so that we let go of it quite naturally in any given moment.

Equanimity is only possible if we are aware of any attachment or aversion we bring to our relationships. We need to be aware of what we are prone to cling to: perhaps our expectations of how others should behave; a belief that our friends should make us happy; or an assumption that others see the world the way we do, sharing the same priorities. When we cling too tightly to our views about how 'proper' friends behave, just watch the suffering that ensues. We tend to assume that another person has hurt us when, in fact, it is our own beliefs and expectations that have made us suffer.

Clinging in our relationships also overlooks the need to cultivate our own inner strength. Dependent on others to validate our existence and make us feel worthwhile and lovable, we cede our sovereignty, along with our capacity to be calm and content. Neediness in our relationships also stands in the way of the natural flow of compassion. It is hard to feel compassion for someone when we resent them for not fulfilling what we believe we need from them. When we are stuck in a simplistic perception of a person as good or bad, it is also difficult to see their behaviour realistically, as the result of all the causes and conditions at play in their life.

EVERYONE IS A STRANGER

Jennifer Taylor is a Buddhist teacher who lives in Alice Springs in the centre of Australia, and exudes all the warmth and peacefulness of the desert. I was on a week-long retreat where she was one of the teachers and I had an opportunity for a half-hour appointment with her in which I could address any aspect of my practice. I decided to seek an opinion on a troubling relationship with a female friend I have known over several decades. I made a full presentation to her of the history of the relationship, complete with revealing anecdotes. I was curious to know whose 'side' Jenny might take, or what advice she might suggest. What would be her answer? Her response, however, was not what I expected: 'You seem to view this relationship in very distinct parcels, all neatly tied up with string. I'm just wondering if you've acknowledged the mystery in the situation?'

As a matter of fact I had not. Not even once.

Over the years that I had chewed over the details of our interactions, mystery could not have been further from my mind. Yet Jenny was right: there was so much in this relationship that I could never know for sure. I was relying on my memories and my fixed view of an unknowable other. How ardently we believe the stories in our heads, as if they are the only version of events. Jenny was asking me to surrender to some not-knowing, to let go of my stories from the past, all my educated guesses and assumptions, and to try to relate to this friend afresh as a new person in each new moment. When we freeze our perceptions of the characters in our lives we blind ourselves to mystery. The longer we have known someone, the higher the danger of seeing them in a fixed way and the more important it becomes to meet them afresh in the present moment.

With people we have known for many years, such as family members, we can stop seeing them with any clarity because we forget to stop and look. When we do finally pause to look at a relation with open, non-judgemental attention we can feel struck by a view that is free of the distortions of our usual needs or self-interest. We find ourselves asking, *Who is this?* in a way that does not seek definitive answers but leaves us open.

With the people in our school community too, how easy it is to overlook the complexity of the other and settle for our fixed views. I have seen others as two-dimensional characters in a B-grade movie:

the villain, the victim, the hero. Or we see others in terms of their faults without acknowledging that the flaws we perceive are often the indicators of the very issues we could benefit from examining in ourselves ('it takes one to know one!'). We can challenge ourselves to see others as more than their different view, or who they vote for, or even how they behaved last time we saw them. For none of these impressions can capture who anybody actually is.

I have found that remaining open to other parents, trying to refrain from labelling, and even letting bygones be bygones has kept relationships alive and full of possibility. There is also an element of relief, along with pleasure, when we bring such openness to our daily encounters with others: it does not feel pleasant to hold a grudge, to dislike another, to intentionally shut somebody out of our life. We feel happier, and even more confident in ourselves, when we can love others freely, and we can do this more easily when, as many a Buddhist puts it, we *get out of our own way*.

GOSSIPING

As a way of reinforcing their commitment to practice, it is common for Zen Buddhists to make a vow that they will not discuss the faults of others. I have heard more than one of them remark, half-joking, on how little there is to talk about in the early days after taking this vow. The vow serves as a statement of serious intention, an expression of commitment to take responsibility for the wholesomeness of their daily speech. If they accidentally break their vow, they bring conscious awareness to the situation and learn from it.

Discussing the faults of others is, for many of us, a temptation that is hard to resist. Or as the late Dorothy Parker would say on social occasions, 'If you don't have anything nice to say, come and sit next to me.' Yet bringing conscious awareness to such a habit can be revealing, as Camilla found.

After a retreat I decided to focus on one aspect of the Buddha's Eightfold Path, and that was skilful speech. At that time I was involved with the pre-school and a lot of mothers in a very competitive neighbourhood. I started to listen to myself more in social settings and realised that most of my speech was negative. I'd hang up the phone or walk away from a conversation feeling uncomfortable. A part of me felt ashamed about my behaviour so I looked more closely at what was going on. I saw that pulling apart someone else made me feel better about myself, my parenting and my kids.

I've noticed now a theme in school classes where there will always be at least one child, maybe two or three, who parents like to criticise and talk about. The child may have some challenging behaviours and we all want to focus on these because we don't want to look at any deficiencies in our own children. The amount of gossiping that was going on in my group reminded me of being in high school. I wanted the flattery of belonging to the in-crowd but I also wanted access to all kinds of information a network of mothers hold. Yet everything was a drama for these mothers, usually based on negativity, but you felt a need to be constantly in the loop.

I could already feel in my body just how horrible it really was, and it just reached a point where something I initially found pleasant started feeling worse and worse. I just wasn't enjoying the relationships so I started to withdraw from that group.

Now I would arrive to pick up the children, see the group and no longer join them, and I stopped speaking on the phone to them. It was then interesting to watch the part of me that still needed acceptance from the group, but that was dwarfed by the huge relief I felt. Interestingly, some of the mothers in that group started what felt like a new relationship with me. I became more open with them about my struggles in parenting and then they became more open. No longer associated with the group, we developed some real friendships.

As is always the case with me and any of the breakthroughs I've had, it was not a matter of telling myself gossiping is wrong. The change came through a close investigation over the course of a month where I asked, 'What is the effect of this gossiping? What is it doing to me? What is it doing to other people?' I imagined being that poor mother who everyone was saying negative things about.

I no longer gossip because I can no longer delude myself about the urge to gossip. I know what it is and I can't hide that truth from myself. Now I see that urge and say, 'Oh Camilla, this is your effort to make you feel good about yourself, or construct a particular self, and you're just trying to solidify it by saying, at least I'm not this other person.' I think with practice we do get to a point where we can't ever go back to that deluded state. We can still engage in the activity but it will never be as pleasant because there is that uncomfortable knowledge of what is really going on.

I found Camilla's report of the mothers at her pre-school surprising as I have found the great majority of mothers I have encountered through child care and school to be the type who have long outgrown any such extreme behaviour—if they were ever capable of it in the first place. That said, however, it is difficult to find someone who absolutely never criticises others, and I have certainly engaged in this dubious pastime myself.

Why do we do it? Discussing others' faults serves our ego in several ways. It strengthens our sense of belonging to an exclusive in-group with its own special standards to uphold. It reinforces our false sense of separation from others, that allows us to feel different, special and superior. As Camilla found, it saves us from confronting any of our own guilt, inadequacy or shame because at least we are not as bad as our enemy. The habit appears to be rewarded in that the social norm is for people to agree with the fault-finder—this serves their own ego and saves the trouble of any disagreement. So we all conspire to stunt each other's personal growth and protect each other's blind spots.

Sure, there are times when someone's behaviour harms others and discussion is helpful to solve the problem. There might be times in our workplace when we need to choose between applicants for a role, where some discussion of their relative strengths and weaknesses is called for. Or we might want to discuss with a close friend how someone has hurt our feelings. The vow is not about adhering to a rule like an ascetic, but to be aware of our intention, for it is quite possible to discuss another's harmful actions with clear awareness of our motive. It does not take much soul-searching to identify whether we are trying to be helpful and constructive or, on the other hand, bolster our ego by criticising someone else.

Whether or not there is much gossiping in our school community, the habit of gratuitously criticising and judging others can begin in the home. One place to be aware of any desire to nit-pick and fault-find is in our living rooms as we watch television as a family. Those popular reality TV shows of the 'talent quest' variety are especially prone to rendering us armchair critics, but if we listen to the way the average family talks about the characters on their screen, then we might seriously question the kind of values our families aspire to. Many of the comments viewers make, in my experience of living rooms, are shallow observations about a character's appearance such that viewers practise disrespect for others based on physical flaws (big nose, fat thighs, dumb voice . . . you know the ones). My family never misses viewing any kind of dance contest so I have heard such remarks from my own loved ones during the early stages of competition—and pounced on them with a moral tirade.

Without awareness, viewers practise gazing on others not compassionately but judgementally, even though the nervous contestants are in fact brave risk-takers who have worked hard to be their best (even if some of them harbour delusions about becoming rich, famous and happy). Still, imagine how compassionate we would feel if the contestant was our own child—why should we not extend the same kind of compassion to other people's children who are equally precious? Moreover, what kind of habits do we want our children to practise: nit-picking and scoffing? Or fairness and kindness?

Tirade finished.

POST-SOCIAL SELF-SEEKING

A hidden part of our social interactions is the way we relive them in our heads. Long after our conversations have ended, we find ourselves minutely examining the exchange in search of a sense of self. *Was I okay? Did I sound silly? Would she think I was boasting? I hope she didn't find me too overwhelming. I wonder if he could tell how nervous I was?* And on and on we might go. From observing her mind throughout a day, Camilla discovered, as most of us potentially could, that she spent an inordinate amount of time analysing her performance in past conversations and in many of her past actions and behaviours, whether they took place a decade ago or a minute ago. Such thoughts arose so often that she invented a label for them, 'historical analysis', to apply to such moments during meditation or throughout her day. In her words:

> Over a two-year period, consciously labelling many of my thought processes as 'historical analysis' helped me become aware of just how often I was reviewing past conversations. I'd also notice that this habit was never particularly pleasant. Seeing this clearly, the whole syndrome just diminished: I used to spend 80 per cent of a meditation sit conducting 'historical analysis', and that reduced to around 10 per cent. It definitely wasn't a matter of telling myself off or even of making a decision to give it up. The habit just went away by itself after deeply observing the unpleasant feelings it created.
>
> In particular, the very distant memories have stopped arising. One in particular, of ganging up with another friend while at high school to bully another girl, really tormented me. It was a constant reminder that my 'self' was a bad one.
>
> My constant historical analysis pointed to a sense of my own insufficiency: I had this need to keep constructing and revising and evaluating my 'self'. I had already faced my childhood issues, such as my alcoholic father, but the habit of self-construction persisted. Then on a retreat it dawned on me that I didn't really need to construct a self at all and I was amazed at the sense of freedom this created in me. It no longer mattered whether the self was 'good', 'bad', 'envious', for it is all a random fabrication. All I have to concern myself with is whatever thought, feeling or mood is manifesting in the present moment.

Camilla also discovered her tendency to give disproportionate attention to remarks that were in fact a non-event. Random, off-the-cuff comments from others could see her reinterpreting, misinterpreting and assuming an ability to read the minds and motives of others. In more lucid moments, Camilla could see in herself that very human tendency to spin simple utterances into highly significant dramas.

Of course, our tendency to perform post-mortems on our conversations is just one of the tools we use to construct a sense of self—always a perilous use of our time, according to the Buddha. 'Historical analysis' tends to feed our self-absorption, if not self-fascination. Camilla applies the Buddha's teaching of not-self.

> When we really buy into having a self that we need to constantly defend from all these attacks, it takes an enormous amount of emotional effort, and a huge toll. So there is liberation in being able to say to ourselves, 'Wow, I don't need to do that; there's nothing to protect.'

Still, reflecting back on our conversations is not always narcissistic, if we do so mindfully and without a need to justify the 'self', as Camilla points out:

> There are times to sit and ponder whether we used words wisely in a past conversation. We do need to take responsibility for our role in conversations, and sometimes mindful reflection can lead us to help someone, to become more sensitive or even apologise. This kind of healthy reflection, though, is a long way from the constant replaying of scenarios in our head where we worry whether our 'self' measures up—which is really useless.

Self-putdowns

Despite the advances of feminism, most women seem to be hard-wired to put themselves down, rarely allowing themselves to own any positive qualities or achievements. One mother, Annica, expressed it like this:

> I went through a patch where I felt a little flat after talking to other mothers and I was curious to know what was behind this feeling. I tried to observe my mood more closely after these conversations and notice any thoughts fuelling it, when I finally saw it. I had been engaging in that highly female activity of putting myself down in front of others. I always seemed to be telling people how disorganised I was, how slack, dull-witted or incompetent. I wasn't the only one, I seemed to be part of a culture of mothers who did this. It wasn't one-upmanship but one-downmanship.
>
> I realised that this couldn't be good for me. I would be appalled to catch myself picking on anyone else in this way, so why do I condone it for myself? And why are women so reluctant to claim what they are doing well at? I recall chatting to several men over the years who have had no qualms about saying, 'I'm good at my job', but it's hard to even imagine a woman doing this. We don't want to be seen as bragging, competing or lording it over others, but do we have to publicly expose our vulnerabilities in such an unbalanced way?
>
> I don't have a problem with self-deprecating humour, but I think many women take that too far and develop a habit of portraying themselves as the bumbling fool, which just feeds our general sense of self-doubt. I decided to be more vigilant about this habit. I would try to stop publicly criticising myself, but if I accidentally fell back into the habit, I would try to add something positive about myself.

Possibly part of the same syndrome, I notice mothers are always saying sorry for minute matters—for accidentally brushing against someone's elbow, for asking the smallest of favours, for having a chance to speak—as though we have to apologise for our existence. It is also common for high-achieving women to quietly confide they feel like a fraud, rushing to claim, 'I'm not a real town planner / lawyer / journalist / researcher / entrepreneur . . . ' Men do not seem to do this. Why do we? What kind of rewards come from selling ourselves short? Did society condition us, as females, to be this way? Probably.

When I ask the women around me why they habitually downplay their strengths, they admit it comes from a perception of how they need to be for others to accept them, as well as a way to avoid envy and competition. Self-effacement may have been effective protection at high school and in early adulthood, surrounded as we were with insecure friends trying to find their place in the world. Yet these days it may be time to dispense with our need to win positive regard from every person we meet. In Buddhist terms, we can let go of that craving for approval which creates suffering. Grasping for approval from others limits our freedom to be ourselves—that is, women with weaknesses but also strengths, with regrets but also achievements, with limitations but also potential. We can aim to see ourselves more realistically, with more balance and fairness, and then present ourselves in the world accordingly.

DUALISTIC THINKING

As mothers of schoolchildren we might see other parents in terms of 'working or at home', 'private or public school', 'mothers of boys or mothers of girls', 'in my clique or not worth talking to', 'a good or bad mother', 'blue or white collar', 'a useful contact or a waste of my time', 'a drinker or non-drinker'. The potential for simplistic divisions between parents is without limit, but are we really so incredibly different so very separate from each other? As any Tibetan Buddhist will tell us, we all have two significant points in common: we all experience suffering and we all want to be happy. Parents, of course, have the added point in common that we want our children to be happy.

One Buddhist who gave up dualistic thinking is Robina Courtin, a Buddhist nun of the Tibetan tradition. In her pre-Buddhist life, she saw all humans in terms of black or white, male or female, rich or poor. Raised in Australia, she is famous for sharing Buddhist teachings with prisoners in the United States, many on death row. On one of her visits home to Australia, I witnessed her addressing an auditorium of three thousand people with no nerves, no notes and plenty of spontaneous humour. She talks at breakneck speed, never stumbling, never lost for a word.

On another occasion I saw Robina speak at a public event, where she explained her journey towards Buddhist practice. To the great amusement of the crowd, she told us about her life before she became a Buddhist: how she started as an Anti-racist, then became a Feminist, then a Lesbian-Feminist, then a Lesbian-Feminist-Separatist who would punch any man who talked to her. Vicki Mackenzie interviewed her for the book *Why Buddhism?*, where Robina describes the epiphany that brought her to Buddhist teachings.

> The compassion I had for black people, was equalled by the anger I had towards white people. And then when I became a feminist my compassion for female people was equalled by the anger I had for male people. That's why, after ten years of being very political and hating first of all the straight people, then all the white people, then all the rich people, then all the male people, there was no one left to blame. I'd exhausted all the possibilities.

My heart meant well but the methodology was a disaster. It just created more violence, more problems. It was so clear.

It was also obvious that my own mind was becoming crazy. I couldn't hate half the human race—it wasn't on. It was logical that it was destroying Robina. At that point I began to listen to the Buddha's teaching—looking at Robina for the first time in my life. I knew that only by looking at Robina's mind, getting rid of the pollution, would I be qualified to help or be of any benefit to the world.

The Buddha warned us to beware of 'dualistic' thinking. We engage in dualistic thinking when we see others in terms of black or white, ignoring any shades of grey such that we dismiss the enormous complexity of a world where change is ceaseless. We engage in dualistic thinking when we see the whole world and its people in terms of pairs of opposites—right / wrong, good / bad, attractive / unattractive—or when we catch ourselves saying, 'There are two types of people in the world . . .'

Being aware of the way we divide people into categories under simplistic labels, and holding our impressions of others more loosely, helps us to see more clearly and be more open to others. Let go of our dualistic views of other parents, teachers and children, and we free ourselves to walk the Buddha's Middle Way through the school playground.

CONNECTING MEANINGFULLY WITH OTHERS

Feeling disconnected from others, or eager to attract more respect or affection, we may have made resolutions to improve ourselves through reading newspapers and books, through travel, study, or through buying the objects that might make ourselves more attractive. We might then feel disappointed when others do not seem particularly interested in the fruits of our efforts. After all, they are engaged in their own quest to attract love and respect—and uphold a self-image.

The answer to this conundrum is to commit to being a *source* of love rather than constantly looking for more love for ourselves. Initiate loving actions towards others, rather than waiting for them to come to you, and witness how much more love begins to flow in all directions. With the intention to cultivate lovingkindness, we face the world with a specific orientation. We may not always achieve our objective to be loving but our inner compass is at least set so we can grow in that direction. Regular practice of lovingkindness meditation, as described in the next chapter, is an effective way to make such a commitment.

For me, a turnaround in my experience of conversation can occur when I switch out of my habitual mode to making conscious awareness the *principal aim* of an encounter. Aware of the present, firmly grounded in my body and closely listening to my companion of the moment, my aim shifts from trying to impress, trying to enjoy myself or trying to gain something for myself onto the safer ground of spiritual practice. In that space of letting go, I am more likely to experience the flow of compassion, skilful speech and openness.

Inquiry

- Are you mindful of the need in each parent you meet to connect, belong and be seen?
- Do you remember that focusing on the social needs of others is an effective way to overcome your own insecurities?
- Have you realised the importance of equanimity—the ability to remain calm and ungrasping throughout the highs and the lows of a friendship?

- Do your expectations and beliefs of how friends should behave make you suffer?
- Can you allow your friends and acquaintances to be imperfect?
- Are you open to the mystery of any relationship, the fact that your perception of it is not necessarily the truth of it?
- If you find yourself gossiping or criticising others, what are your motives?
- How much time do you spend reviewing past conversations? Is it a habit you could let go of to some degree?
- Do you habitually put yourself down in front of others? What are your reasons?
- Do you perceive the other parents you meet in dualistic or extreme terms that overlook the complexity of any individual?
- Are you a source of love or just looking for it?
- Have you ever considered making conscious awareness the primary aim of any conversation?

CHAPTER 6

sharing

A MOTHER WHO FINDS BUDDHIST teachings helpful may feel moved to share them with her children. She might want to help her children manage their emotions, address negativity, increase their self-awareness or cultivate calm and contentment. She may be seeking to establish a shared system of values, honouring virtues such as compassion, kindness and gratitude. Discussing the teachings with her children is a way to create experiences of intimacy and sharing. The more a mother and child practise exploring weighty issues together, the stronger the bonds of communication become.

Sharing Buddhist teachings with her children might be a mother's way to teach her child that constantly seeking more than we already have is not the path to happiness. The media constantly blares the messages: you do not have enough, life can be better, you can be better, you need to buy more, you need to *be* more. The Buddha's message is the antidote to this way of thinking for the Buddha taught that all this craving is exactly what makes us unhappy. Sharing an alternative way of being in the world, a way that helps us to be happy with less, shows our children how it is possible to turn inward for satisfaction, rather than relying too heavily on the world outside us.

Yet where would you start? Or more importantly, how would you start—with what kind of attitude? The answer, not surprisingly, can only be: softly, softly. Perhaps the best advice comes from Thich Nhat Hanh's third Mindfulness Training, which addresses the importance of avoiding attachment to views.

> Aware of the suffering brought about when we impose our views on others, we are committed not to force others, even our children, by any means whatsoever . . . to adopt our views. We will respect the right of others to be different and to choose what to believe and how to decide.

So we share the teachings with our children in a way, and at a pace, that recognises their level of interest. Alex, for example, is only six and is yet to show any interest in Buddhism, so I have not discussed it with him at all. Zac, on the other hand, has been interested in the various interpretations of the meaning of life from a young age and has always asked questions. Sharing the teachings with him, whether we are meditating together or discussing the teachings themselves, has provided a long stream of precious, and priceless, parenting moments.

What to share

Some mothers commit to regular sharing of the teachings with their children through meditating or reading stories together. One mother, Edith, was concerned about signs of low self-esteem in her troubled young son. To make the teaching about Buddha Nature memorable she bought him a black rock from a crystal shop to keep at his bedside: while the exterior appeared rough and bumpy (as many people can appear from the outside), the interior was shining and luminous (as we all are on the inside once delusions are peeled away). I found this such a touching way of telling him that she believed in his essential goodness come what may.

We can also share Buddhist teachings on a more spontaneous basis, as part of our daily conversations with our children. Buddhist mother of three Fiona Clarke is in an excellent position to guide us about which teachings we might share with our children. She has been teaching Buddhism as a scripture teacher at her local school for the past seven years as well as helping to organise a children's program for Rigpa, the school headed by the teacher Sogyal Rinpoche. On the annual Rigpa retreat, held over ten days each January, she plays a key role in running sessions for up to eighty children and teens.

I attended an inspiring talk Fiona delivered to a room of Buddhist scripture teachers where she shared a list of 'key understandings' that children could take from Buddhism:

We are all fundamentally good

Every one of us, without exception, has at our core Buddha Nature—described as an innate wisdom, fundamental goodness or enlightened essence. Fiona laments she meets children who already believe they are bad. She strives to teach them *they are not their behaviour*, nor are they what others tell them they are. Of course, children still need to learn to take responsibility for their behaviour and feel genuine heartfelt regret when they have hurt others, but with knowledge of their Buddha Nature they recognise that *they* are good but *their actions* were not. They learn to believe in their own essential goodness.

Being kind makes you happy

When we catch our children being kind, we can ask them how it feels inside. We can ask them to compare that feeling to the one they experience when they are not so kind. We live in a society that habitually rewards academic or sporting achievement, yet so often overlooks acts of kindness, generosity or forgiveness. As our children talk to us about their day, there are plenty of opportunities to reinforce the value of kindness. We can teach them to appreciate the generosity of others, understand those who have wronged them and feel for those who suffer.

There are many different ways to look at a situation

We can *choose* how we react to each event in our day. Fiona discusses the situation where another child has hurt ours. 'If our children have always retaliated without thinking, they can gradually train themselves to react in another way. There is a moment between getting hurt and lashing back at the other person.' We need to make skilful use of that moment by learning how to pause. Teaching our children to meditate is one way to enhance the skill of pausing so that they can calm themselves and then think more clearly.

Fiona takes every opportunity to teach empathy:

> It is very important for children to come to understand others' point of view, to 'stand in someone else's shoes' to see what it is like for them. We can ask them when they have a disagreement with another child, for example, what they think was happening for the other person, how they think the other is feeling.

Everyone seeks inner peace and contentment

Understanding that everyone is trying to be happy and avoid suffering leads to tolerance of others, and their behaviour, as well as a sense of how much we all have in common. Fiona emphasises the need to understand that happiness can be short term or long term, and that it is best to favour activities that lead to long-term happiness. It is useful to brainstorm with your child activities for each category: for example, short-term happiness can come from lollies, a good movie, or even provoking a sibling.

Fiona lists some sources of long-term happiness:

- attending to our inner world rather than only what is outside us
- regularly remembering the preciousness of our lives
- practising acts of kindness
- behaving ethically
- developing our capacity to let go of negative emotions
- connecting with our inner goodness
- growing wiser and seeing more clearly.

In Fiona's experience, children are generally wise at knowing the difference between short- and long-term sources of happiness, and have identified for Fiona long-term sources such as: 'love, friendship, family, meditation, being peaceful and being in nature.'

Expect change

Challenge your child to think of one thing in the world that does not change. We live in a world where change is the only thing we can really rely on. Whatever has a beginning also has an end. Any understanding of impermanence leads to appreciation and gratitude for what we have, for every person, object or moment can only be with us temporarily.

Since everything changes, it is best to avoid any unhealthy, grasping attachment to any particular object. Toys will break, batteries run out, best friends change, pets die. So we can love our family, friends and pets fully, but with the awareness that things change. As Fiona explains, this is a purer love that does not expect things to always go our way, but accepts with an open heart the way things are. Courage is therefore a component of love, for change and loss are inevitable. We can help our children by reminding them of the truth of impermanence often, so teaching them to expect it and accept it.

Reflect on the world and self-reflect

Our children can run their whole lives on automatic pilot, following their every impulse and believing everything they are told, or they can develop an ability to question, to pause and think deeply about the world and their role in it. We can help our child to develop a habit of questioning the media and its messages, the peer group and its messages, and the whole way the world operates.

The Buddha emphasised the importance of 'knowing in yourselves' what is right rather than blindly following. As mothers, we seek ways of allowing our child to connect with their inner sense of what harms and what helps, by encouraging activities such as discussion, meditation, diary writing, or quiet times of reflection and questioning.

Everything we do, say and think is important

How we decide to use each moment is important, not only because our time is limited but also because of our karma. Everything we do, say and think has the potential to become a habit: each time we think petty thoughts about others, behave selfishly or snap at somebody, we increase the chances that we will do so again. With every act we condition ourselves until we eventually have a certain kind of character. We all have the power to change our trajectory by making wise choices about how to use each moment.

Fiona emphasises that the intention behind each of our actions is also of paramount importance:

> It is not the size of the action, or how the action appears, that matters, but what is in your heart, or why you are doing it. For example, are we helping another because we care about them, or to impress others?

Understand how meditation can help us

An ability to appreciate the value of silence and stillness will serve our children well. Meditating can help our children calm themselves, create perspective in their lives and connect to their own inner peace and wisdom. With time, they learn to rely more on themselves. To enjoy meditation is to realise that happiness does not need to come from endless sources of stimulation outside us. Our children learn an alternative way to be in the world, a way marked by simplicity, a way that counteracts stress, anxiety and conformity.

MEDITATING WITH CHILDREN

The main way I share the teachings with my boys is by guiding them through a meditation as they lie in their beds after their nightly reading session. Of course, I would not dream of forcing a meditation on them, but these days Zac is sure to request one. Our child need not be any particular type of person to enjoy meditating: Zac would never stand out as an especially spiritual type—his interests in life are mainstream and, for the most part, typical of boys his age. Alex is welcome to meditate with us but, being younger, often ends up fidgeting or drifting off into his own imagination—and I leave him to his journey.

Each night I tell Zac, if he is ready for bed on time and has spent enough time on his reading, I will bring my cushion into his bedroom and meditate with him as a reward. Sometimes I am too tired to spend another minute with the boys and they miss out, but usually it is a way for me to enjoy additional meditation time myself and wind down. One night I recorded the meditation so that Zac could listen to it when I am either too exhausted or not home. Many mothers could find a meditation lulls their children into sleep, and I wish I could say the same for my children who have always taken a long time to fall asleep.

The meditation technique I use is the classic one for insomniacs, usually referred to as a 'body scan'. Most mothers with any meditation experience will be familiar with the technique of gradually working through each muscle group from head to toe, choosing the level of detail according to how much time and energy you can summon. The idea initially is to go from general awareness of the present to more specific awareness of parts of the body. This is the wording I tend to go with as Zac lies in his bed. I speak slowly, with plenty of pauses, but it is simple enough for any mother to use her own words.

Very gently close your eyelids, without shutting them tightly, and make sure all the muscles around your eyes are soft and relaxed. No tension at all . . .

Take some moments to listen to each of the tiny sounds of the house. What do you hear?

Imagine your body as it is, lying in a warm bed, in a room, in a house, in a street . . .

Now bring your awareness into your body and see how it feels lying in that warm bed, surrendering to the power of gravity.

Take some moments to hear your breathing, feel your breathing, to feel the mattress, your pajamas, the doona.

Now we are ready to bring our attention to the face and make sure it is completely relaxed: imagine that it is melting butter . . . softening.

Make sure your jaw is slack, your forehead is not frowning, your tongue is at rest.

Notice the cold air flowing into your nostrils and the warm air coming out.

Now bring your attention to your neck and shoulders, and see that they are floppy and loose like a ragdoll's.

Moving your attention down your arms, check in with each muscle and notice any sensations. Release any tension.

Spend some time being aware of your hands and fingers. What sensations can you feel? You might even think to thank your hands for all the ways they help you throughout your day . . .

One does feel virtuous after guiding one's children through a meditation. Quite a guilt-buster, meditation is definitely 'quality time' together, and if I die tomorrow, at least I will have taught the boys one reliable skill in self-soothing. One night I asked Zac how he felt after a meditation. His answer delighted me: 'Relaxed, of course . . . and happy for no reason.' This was more than adequate compensation for the fact that he was still not asleep.

Sometimes Zac and I do a lovingkindness meditation at bedtime, which Zac also describes as 'very relaxing'. This meditation creates good karma for Zac as it helps to create the conditions for him to be a kind, loving person. I might start this meditation with him in a similar way to the one above, focusing on quietening down the mind and relaxing the body, before launching into the lovingkindness meditation itself.

The usual order for this meditation is to start by wishing yourself well, then to do the same for somebody you love, followed by a neutral person who you do not know very well and then someone you find difficult to love. We guide our child through the meditation, speaking slowly and treating the experience as a meditation for ourselves as well as our child. The precise wording is not particularly important, but here is a guide:

Now, focusing on your own body, using all your heart, wish yourself well:
    May I be well
    May I be free from suffering
    May I be happy
    May I be safe.

Now picture in your mind's eye somebody you love, maybe Dad, maybe Grandpa, and wish them well:
    May he be well
    May he be free from suffering
    May he feel deep peace
    May he be happy.

Now take this beautiful feeling you have for the person you love and spread it across to somebody you do not know so well. You might choose one of the teachers at school, or the lady who lives across the road:

> May she be well
> May she be free from suffering
> May she feel calm and peaceful
> May she be content.

Now we're going to do something tricky and picture somebody we find difficult to like. We are going to try and remember that they also want to be happy just like us. And they too suffer in this world, just like us:

> May he be well
> May he be free from suffering
> May he feel relaxed
> May he be happy and peaceful.

We are at the point in our meditation when we are ready to send lovingkindness to millions of other living beings.

Take this feeling of love and send it to everyone in this house: May our family be happy and safe.

Now think of all your friends: May they all be happy and well.

Picture now your whole school: May every child, teacher and parent be happy and well.

May everybody in Sydney be happy and safe.

May everybody in Australia be happy and safe.

May all living beings, in all directions, all over the world, be happy and at peace.

Occasionally I will add during either of these meditations the words: *Do not worry if your mind wanders away with some thoughts—everyone's mind does that sometimes. Just patiently bring your attention back to our meditation.* We don't want to present meditation as a discipline, nor as yet another tool in their life for self-evaluation. Ensure they experience the whole process as gentle and nurturing.

While your children may be different, Zac has never been a fan of solitary activities so meditation does tend to be an activity we do together. Then again, if he ever feels anxious or fearful at night, or cannot fall asleep, I advise him to meditate as he lies in his bed, and this is often precisely the medicine he needs to halt a flow of anxious thoughts or stories and fall asleep. For that matter, it is often exactly what his mother needs to block unhelpful thoughts and fall asleep.

My approach of guiding the boys through a meditation as they lie in bed is what has evolved for my family, but is not necessarily the conventional approach. Other children might seek a more formal or regular approach. Your child might be open to creating a shrine or altar to sit before, or to sit on a cushion and assume the correct posture. After initially guiding your child through a couple of meditations, your child may be ready to meditate independently.

I finally erected a small altar in our spare room where I meditate, complete with candle, incense, Buddha statues and objects from nature. The boys enjoyed helping me create it but are yet to visit it with any regularity. Marek, on the other hand, has been pleading with me to take it down ever since, shaking his head every time he looks at it. He finds it 'seriously weird'. Which amuses me.

Another meditation technique that many children find peaceful is to sit and concentrate on the flame of a candle. The first time Zac tried this, in a meditation hall, he meditated for over half an hour and even went back later in the day for another sit. Watching the smoke from burning incense has also been very settling for both Zac and Alex. So if your family were to set up an altar to meditate before, candles and incense are definitely simple attractions to add.

Fiona raises an important point about teaching children to meditate:

> A common misconception about meditation among children— and adults for that matter—is that we are aiming to stop our mind from thinking. We might as well try to stop a river from flowing. Meditation is not about having no thoughts; it is about not being distracted by our thoughts, just noticing them coming and letting them go.

As we may have discovered from our own experience of meditation, it is neither relaxing nor enjoyable when your aim is to stop thinking. This only creates tension, strain and frustration with ourselves. Meditation becomes another way to evaluate ourselves and we lose sight of its real benefits: increasing our ability to practise conscious awareness, cultivating calm, and helping us to understand ourselves and others so that we can meet everyone with compassion.

TEACHING GRATITUDE

Unlike the Buddha's father who tried to hide all the suffering in the world from his son, Fiona believes we need to do the opposite: 'It is really important for our very privileged children to have an understanding of the suffering that exists in the world, to develop both compassion as well as a deep appreciation of how lucky they are.' Her words chime with those of Thich Nhat Hanh, whose fourth Mindfulness Training is called 'Awareness of Suffering': 'Aware that looking deeply at the nature of suffering can help us develop compassion and find ways out of suffering, we are determined not to avoid or close our eyes before suffering.'

Yet Buddhism is never about inflexibility and slavish following of rules or teachers' advice. If we happen to have a child who finds accounts of the suffering in the world deeply distressing, we may understandably choose to protect them from such information until they are older. Similarly, if we ourselves suffer from depression, or other mental health issues, we might also decide that consuming the daily news is not in our best interests. I know several women, Buddhist and non-Buddhist, who have decided to specifically avoid tuning in to world news, as a way to protect their mental health. Fiona would qualify this however:

> While we would accept that avoiding the news is a very valid way to cope initially, we would work on building up the mental strength to eventually be able to cope with anything, rather than continue to live with a level of aversion or fear or a sense of helplessness. In the end, it is very difficult to shut it all out anyway! As our mind strength gradually develops, the upsetting stories then become opportunities to practise for others, and to open our hearts. Of course, this can take a long time, but we are gradually able to cope with a little more, and this gives such a sense of growth and of strength.

Like most mothers, I want to teach my sons to be grateful and aware of how fortunate they are. Zac and Alex can grow jaded at my reports of how most world inhabitants live but I will continue to remind them. Every year UNICEF release a report called *The State of the World's Children*. The report for 2008 revealed that 26,000 children under the age of five die every day, mostly from preventable diseases—although this figure has halved since 1960, it still tells a story of unimaginable suffering.

The State of the World's Children 2006 report focuses on 'excluded and invisible' children, and informs us that:

- 143 million children in the developing world are orphans
- tens of millions of children live on the streets
- 250,000 children are child soldiers
- one in every three girls in developing countries are married by the time they are eighteen
- 171 million children—of which 73 million are under ten years old—are working in hazardous situations or conditions, and
- millions of children toil in private homes as domestic servants.

All these children are incredibly vulnerable to abuse in all its forms.

As any mother realises, we share such information judiciously with consideration for our child's age and maturity. Often enough, opportunities to remind our children of certain facts about the world arise in the natural flow of family life: for example, when our children complain about their chores it is an ideal time to inform them of the millions of children who cannot even go to school, nor experience a childhood, because they are employed as domestic servants far from their homes. If they complain about school, tell them about child labour. If they complain about how bored they are, tell them about child soldiers. The 2006 report, easily downloadable from the internet, certainly has all the details as well as photo essays and videos.

Awareness, through frequent reminders, of how so many children their age live, helps our children to know how fortunate they are. Gratitude is an excellent antidote to our perpetual wanting of more than we have. Only when we realise how abundantly blessed we already are can we act on the Buddha's Second Noble Truth: 'Desires cause suffering so let them go.' We can challenge our children by asking them to compare the feeling of 'wanting' with the feeling of 'appreciating'. Does it feel good inside when you want something really strongly? How does it feel, in comparison, when you understand the value of all the gifts and treasures in your life?

Another reason it helps children to be aware of suffering in the world is that it helps to bring perspective to their own problems. We know ourselves when we hear how difficult life can be for others that we begin to question why we ever worried so much about some of our more trifling problems. The larger our view of the world, the more we realise the truth of our privileged status, living as we do in relative comfort and security. A larger world view might bring our children to hesitate before committing to some of their more ridiculous remarks: *I've got the worst family in the world! Everybody's house is better than mine! Stop treating me like your slave! Everyone has more toys than I do!*

As with any lesson, if we can build it into the structure of our day, the message sinks in more deeply. Whenever we have a family dinner with all four of us present we join hands, close our eyes and speak those traditional words: *For what we are about to receive, may our hearts be truly thankful.* Once or twice I have started a discussion about how many people were involved in bringing this meal to our table. We could list the farmers, the truck drivers, the wholesalers, the shop owners, the shop workers, and then all the people who support these workers: their families, their doctors, their nurses, their council workers. Eventually it becomes clear that we need to be grateful to millions of people. Such discussions are teachings in interconnectedness.

Even Marek supports our ritual of 'grace' or 'giving thanks', agreeing that he wants the boys to grow up with a sense of appreciation rather than taking everything for granted. Although, to be honest, young

Alex will often try to sabotage the ritual by groaning and intoning, 'Grace is for hippies!' Still, after rolling his eyes, he usually joins in.

FINDING OPPORTUNITIES IN DAILY LIFE

Zac has to deliver a two-minute speech for the public-speaking competition at school. With only three days left to prepare I suggest he starts work, but he feels overwhelmed, declaring: 'I can't do it. It's impossible. I hate writing speeches. I suck at it. My speech will be the worst in the class.' He is utterly despondent. The night before he is to deliver the speech we have worked hard and now he feels confident, 'I can't wait to give my speech tomorrow,' he chirps. I try to take him back to his earlier attitude as a way to teach him how misleading our darker moods can turn out to be. I point out that everything he so strongly believed when in that mood turned out to be wrong.

Rather than do his thinking for him I asked him questions about his dark mood of a few days ago: Did it help the process for you to believe those thoughts and surrender to that mood? What have you learned about doing projects like this? He proceeded to apologise and feel ashamed of himself, but I told him I was not asking him these questions to shame him. I was able to explain that most people feel a little anxious and overwhelmed at the beginning of a large project and that it is not wrong to feel that way. We just need to be careful that we don't allow ourselves to become too swept up in strong emotions, believing their lies.

Through this experience I was able to talk about the Buddha's teaching of impermanence and how all our emotions arise only to pass away. They will not hang around forever, no matter how strong they feel at the time. I was able to teach him that feeling strong emotions is never 'wrong' but that what is important is how we deal with them.

We were able to identify the risk of putting yourself down and being cruel to yourself in times of stress, and acknowledge that this was not helpful to the job at hand. Importantly, Zac was able to see from his own experience the way thoughts and predictions, formulated while in a dark mood, were so inaccurate and unhelpful. Having debriefed the experience thoroughly, I have since been able to remind him of the lessons we identified when similar situations have arisen.

As Fiona mentioned earlier in the chapter, empathy is another value we can teach in the course of our daily conversations with children. It is also worth making a habit of discussing other people's feelings. We can ask, 'How do you think Jack feels when you say you hate him?' or, 'What do you think it is like for Dad when you talk like that?' When they tell us about incidents at school we can ask questions about how people were feeling. We can even point to people in the media—on TV and in magazines—and ask our children to interpret their feelings. It helps to build up a shared vocabulary for feelings, to talk about feelings regularly and to notice the feelings of others. In fact, such behaviours are essential to developing emotional intelligence.

PRACTISING APPRECIATION OF NATURE

Nature—the bush, the beach, the park or our own backyard—is a place where we find that our capacity to be calm, open and present multiplies. Absorbing the beauty of a natural landscape, we are more likely to relax and rediscover an acceptance of the present moment in which we halt the usual stream of desires and want nothing more. A popular feature on the calendar of my Buddhist group, albeit *sans* children, is the silent bushwalk where we all walk together without talking for a couple of hours before selecting a spot in nature to meditate together. We then break the silence for a lunch with a glorious valley view.

A love of the outdoors and appreciation of the natural world is one of the greatest gifts we can bestow on our children, a gift that only their parents, or other adults in their lives, can give them. Allowing time for children to play outdoors is a chance to teach them a simple kind of happiness, that is as accessible as walking out the front door or down the road. Modern children spend so much time pressing buttons in front of screens that these days it is not unusual to meet children who spend hardly any time in nature. I have been amazed taking young children on bushwalks to hear that they feel 'scared', their lack of experience in nature rendering it eerie for them.

I remember looking forward to family bushwalks as a child, yet my own children and many of their peers turn up their noses at the prospect, or flatly refuse to go. They always enjoy a bushwalk with friends once it is under way, but there are so many indoor options to compete with such natural pleasures. Lamenting this tendency, my family has banded together with a group of five or so local families to do a group bushwalk once a month. The children are more likely to be keen when their friends accompany them, and as parents we create happy childhood memories in nature.

One way to nurture an appreciation in our children is to share our own. Show them our own joy over the beauty of the trees, the flowers, the sunset. It is so moving when they follow our example and point out the perfect hibiscus or the colourful butterfly. Marvel at insects and examine together leaves and other objects in fine detail. Ask them questions to activate the sense doors: *What does this tree smell like? What noises can you hear? How does that breeze feel on your face? Can you see anything you've never seen before? What colours can you see in this leaf?* Some parents encourage their children to sketch objects they find in nature as an opportunity to practise a deep looking they might rarely undertake in their daily lives.

Children love playing imaginatively in nature, and their resourcefulness and creativity in the outdoors is inspiring. Children are quite naturally aware and curious. In our busy lives, the challenge lies in creating the opportunities.

KNOWING IS OVERRATED

Besides Buddhist teachings, we of course share all kinds of knowledge with our children about morality, about human nature and the world in general. This is our job. Being older, 'wiser', bigger and stronger than my sons, at least for the time being, I have occasionally caught myself on somewhat of an ego-trip in their presence. They inquire about some aspect of life, and I instantly puff up with pride and proceed to hold forth. I will tell them how to think because I'm a wise grown-up who knows absolutely everything.

For now, they believe I know the answers and, chuffed by such flattery, I assume for a few glorious moments that I do. I forget that maybe they are wiser than me, in that it is wiser to question than to know. In Buddhism, not knowing is a far more spiritually advanced state than knowing, not to mention being the fast-track to that treasured quality known as humility.

We live in a culture where 'knowing'—knowledge, information and answers—is highly valued. We have been taught to feel insecure and inadequate when we do not know everything about our situation. We have been taught to value ourselves for what we know, what we have learned. We feel good about ourselves when we feel we know something with certainty, when we are the one who can present 'the facts'. We define wisdom, in our culture, as 'having all the answers'.

About ten years ago, when I was pregnant with my firstborn, I participated in a course to become a Lifeline telephone counsellor. This was naive of me because, as soon as I became a breast-feeding mother, I became completely unavailable for the four-hour shifts required. Still, I benefitted from doing the course, which involved either observing or playing the part of counsellor in numerous role-plays where trainers rated our performance. Where just about everyone fell down was when a caller phoned with a problem and, as beginners, our reflex was to jump straight in with a solution: 'Have you tried . . . ?' Most of us felt obliged to fix the problem. Yet if we were being trained to actually solve callers' problems, then each of us would have to be extremely knowledgeable about an immeasurable range of social issues.

So the course facilitator faced a considerable challenge in deprogramming us all with words to the effect of: *Don't fix their problem. Listen, identify their feelings, provide the space for the caller to feel heard and understood and, only after doing that, ask questions that empower them to come up with their own options.* So, as trainee counsellors, we needed to learn to sit down for a session thinking not, 'I'm the counsellor so I know', but rather, 'I'm the counsellor so I *don't* know'.

As parents, we pressure ourselves to know everything, to know what to do and say in every situation. I have a hunch that what has irritated teens and young adults most about their parents, through the ages, might be the common tendency to 'know it all'. After all, it carries the assumption that the child knows little.

Knowing it all is about rigidity in our views, a lack of openness, a lack of willingness to learn or grow ourselves. A great attraction of Buddhist teachings for me is that wisdom is about questions rather than answers. Buddhists strive to cultivate a spirit of inquiry, openness and curiosity. We avoid living on automatic pilot and relying on past experiences to tell us how to be now, and rather strive to pay attention and notice *what is*.

Knowing it all stops a parent from listening, leaving their child feeling unheard or misunderstood. We know when we have problems ourselves that we would rather discuss them with a friend who will ask us questions and explore the issues with us than a friend who 'knows everything', who instantly gives us advice before they have heard the details.

We live in a hierarchical society, where children find themselves at the bottom of the heap. Certain teachers and parents in every school environment talk to children with such a lack of respect, or even politeness, that onlookers cringe. As adults we routinely assume ourselves to be superior beings, but this is worth questioning. Adults may have a better idea of how society expects us to behave and a better ability to follow those rules, yet a child might, in any given situation, be just as much, if not more, compassionate, generous, kind or open than an adult.

Inquiry

- Do you expect your children to adopt your views or do you allow them some freedom to choose?
- Could you work some Buddhist lessons into your daily conversations with children? For example:
  - We are all fundamentally good.
  - Being kind makes you happy.
  - There are many ways to look at a situation.
  - Everyone is trying to be happy and avoid suffering.
  - Expect change.
  - Reflect rather than settle for automatic pilot.
  - Everything we do, say and think is important.

- Meditation is a way to reconnect to yourself and your inner voice.
- If your child is interested, when might be the best time in your week to practise some meditation together? Would you consider setting up an altar with candles and incense?
- Is your child aware of suffering in the world so that they can learn compassion but also gratitude for what they have and perspective on their own problems?
- Do you debrief emotional outbursts, using them to demonstrate how all emotions pass away and the importance of dealing with them in ways that avoid harm?
- Do you teach your child to dispute the thoughts that arise from dark moods?
- Do you teach your child to treat themselves at such times compassionately rather than harshly?
- Do you share the joy of nature with your children? Have they enjoyed ample opportunities to discover the delights of the outdoors?
- Do you allow yourself to occasionally feel comfortable with 'not knowing'? Have you learned to value questions more than answers?

CHAPTER 7

fear

As Zac and Alex grow older, I feel my love for them increase with each passing day. These glorious feelings of adoration, however, are tinged with *dukkha*, a nagging sense of unease. The mounting love is accompanied by a rising fear that they might suffer or, even worse, that I might somehow lose them. The more I love them, the more vulnerable to the unexpected I sometimes feel. To a point, fear can be healthy and useful, inducing us to anticipate problems, make practical contingency plans and prepare for the worst. Yet for many, fear and anxiety can take over and debilitate us.

Perhaps it is that I belong to a generation of parents plagued by fears. Our sense of stranger danger, for instance, has radically changed the experience of childhood: today's children have lost the freedom to walk to school, roam the neighbourhood or play unsupervised. Our youngest children play in padded, enclosed indoor playgrounds while many of our older ones would not dream of walking anywhere. We have heard the theories: we have fewer children these days so cannot afford to lose any; and our airwaves are replete with media reports creating an exaggerated sense of the frequency of kidnappings and other crimes against children. Occasionally we read an article explaining that there has been no particular increase in the number of crimes against children, and that most incidents occur within families rather than out on the streets, but our collective fear has skyrocketed regardless.

I have felt my own fears escalate by the practice among parents of sending out group-emails whenever anybody suspect has been noticed in the neighbourhood, whenever a missing child is being searched for, or whenever a new danger has been discovered, be it a carcinogen or a child-unfriendly product. While such emails are sent with the best of intentions, the subtext being 'Let's all be careful!', they also heighten our awareness of danger and fuel our over-protectiveness. The challenge for the mother aspiring to mindful parenting is to be aware of our fears without buying into them so much. Having a fearful thought does not increase the chances of the fearsome event occurring. It can be hair-raising to watch our children cycle so fast, climb so high or wrestle so heedlessly, but we need to spare our children from the effects of our more excessive anxieties.

FEARS GONE TOO FAR

I recently talked to a father, Chris, who had just resigned as a scout leader after over a decade of service. I was surprised because last time I had talked to him he had sounded so passionate about this work. I asked him what had driven him to quit. His answer:

One of the main reasons I resigned was that the mothers were driving me nuts. Some of the fathers too but mainly the mothers. Scouts is about building independence and resourcefulness, about giving boys responsibilities and challenges to solve. The other day we were setting off for a bushwalk and I wanted the boys to sort out what items from their bags to bring along and which items to leave in the hall. The group of mothers loitering in the corner sprang into action to sort out their sons' backpacks. Feeling a little irritated, I yelled above the ruckus, 'Could all the mothers please leave the hall.' One mother was in tears over this request!

Then I set the boys a series of challenges which involved several excursions on public transport. They needed to catch buses, trains and ferries as well as do some walking without adults to supervise them. They were definitely old enough to cope with this level of responsibility but several mothers rang me to say their sons would not be participating. It's my view that we are ruining this generation of children with our mollycoddling. Many have become incapable of doing anything for themselves.

There may be layers of unexplored complexity to this report concerning why the various mothers behaved the way they did, but Chris has a point about our generation of parents. Our concern for the safety of our children has perhaps gone a little too far.

Anne Cassidy, author of *Parents Who Think Too Much*, also worries about the way safety has become such an obsession for our generation. She claims our efforts to keep our children safe and protect them from so many situations not only reinforces debilitating fear and anxiety in ourselves but robs our children of their independence. Children miss out on many of life's most basic experiences due to our fear that they might suffer. To counteract her own tendency to overprotect her three daughters she purposely makes space for experiences that are less than perfectly comfortable, such as walking home from school:

> I'm more likely to make our kids walk in the rain and the cold than in pleasant weather. It's not just plain contrariness. It's because I want them to have a little hardship in their lives. I want them to know discomfort if for no other reason than to appreciate comfort when they have it. Yes, there are limitations. I cannot send the girls to the store for a quart of milk; the store is miles away down a busy, four-lane road. But I can make countless small decisions that will let them know that although their lives are safe, they are not always going to be easy.

I too worry that one of my greatest failings as a parent might be allowing my children to lead lives too free of discomfort and the character-building opportunities that only difficulty can bring.

Without hurdles to overcome, how will my sons develop resilience, resourcefulness, confidence, courage, judgement and, not least, compassion for others who suffer? Of course, nothing will protect them from suffering in the long-run because it is inevitable, but perhaps we do our children a disservice if we deny them all opportunities to practise for what their future lives must, at various points, present.

A wise friend whose now-grown child went through several of the most dreadful of health scares in his teenage years emailed these comments to me:

> He thinks his depth of being is significantly greater than that of many of his friends . . . I have seen the strength and self-understanding and also the real love of life that has come from his suffering.

Circumstances may force our children to suffer, but this might just strengthen them enough to more completely fulfil their potential.

ACCEPT SOME SCRAPES

Recently at a soccer field, the younger brothers and sisters of the players, including my Alex, decided to climb on top of a two-metre concrete tank to play at a height. Perfect, I thought to myself, now I can watch Zac play while Alex remains in view and occupied. The odd nervous parent stood guard at the foot of the tank, watching the situation, but suddenly one mother turned up and ordered her son down. Her son refused—he did not want to be the only one excluded. A great scene blew up with the mother and father shouting and ordering him down. Other parents felt nervous: should they too call their children down in support?

When the boy finally climbed down he was wailing and was immediately smacked. I felt dreadful for the boy, and I also felt guilty that maybe I should have hauled my son down from this potentially dangerous height as well. Had I been selfish and slack in wanting to watch Zac's game in peace, willing to risk Alex's safety to do so? Had I been too lazy to face an argument with Alex? With hindsight, however, I am glad I allowed Alex to stay on the tank. While providing any necessary protection or boundaries, I would like to rebel against the 'extreme-caution' movement that poses a threat to what many would argue are the basic rights of childhood. After all, I spent many hours of my childhood high up in tree-tops, way further than two metres from the ground. Once I fell and broke my wrist but, in retrospect, that injury was worth all those carefree hours.

The challenge is to use our intuition to find the point of balance between protecting our children and allowing them enough freedom to explore their world. Children may suffer the occasional injury, or mishap, but we can challenge ourselves to see this as a normal part of childhood rather than a disaster to beat ourselves up about. Do we have an unconscious belief that such things must not happen, that any pain is somehow wrong or unnatural? Do we believe that we can remove from life anything we do not like? If we do, then we will be unable to bring any tolerance to those numerous parts of our lives that are not perfect. A significant proportion of life is beyond our control, and as long as we insist this be otherwise we create stress for ourselves. It pays to remember the Buddha's First Noble Truth: 'There is suffering and unsatisfactoriness.'

Many of us need to acknowledge our tendency towards being overprotective, and practise restraint so that we raise neither nervous wrecks nor frustrated rebels.

A client in his seventies for whom I was writing a biography reminded me of how much childhood has changed. He reported that a 'riderless horse' would often turn up at his farmhouse. Half an hour later he would arrive home on foot, dirty and grazed. His mother's reaction? Every time she just smiled and told her son, 'You have to fall off a horse nine times before you can call yourself a rider.'

OVERRELYING ON EXTERNAL CONDITIONS

Of course, not all our fears relate to our children. We have plenty for ourselves as well: fear of failure, of not measuring up, of loneliness, of the unforeseen, of aging and of death. We feel uncomfortable with uncertainty and go to great lengths to set up situations of security that render suffering unlikely. While this is wise to a point, we tend to take it too far. We do need some money, but we don't need to sacrifice all balance in our lives to earn vast amounts. We do need some friends, but do we need every single person to like us? We do need some self-confidence, but we can forfeit considerable energy and self-sufficiency by constantly seeking approval and positive feedback from the world outside us.

We create the conditions for fear and anxiety when we insist that the world be a certain way or that life go according to our plans. When we tell ourselves that we must have x, y and z in order to be happy, then any threats to x, y and z trigger our fear. Attached and clinging to too many of our preferences, we come to experience anxiety. Moreover, with change the only constant in life, even if we obtain an object of our desires, we cannot hold onto it forever. Even if we manage to hold onto an object for many years, we feel less excited about it as time passes. We need to reconnect to our inner wisdom, which can answer the question: What do I really need and what am I merely telling myself I need? How much more content, and fearless, we could be if we were capable of seeing the difference between needs and wants, and noticing the abundance of what we already have.

Camilla, like many who have looked deeply into their strongest reactive emotions, has found fear to be what fuels all of them: fear of losing control, fear of falling short as a mother, of being judged, of what the future may hold, and fear of any attack on her constructed concept of a self. Camilla, like many Buddhists, has made a vow to live fearlessly, to never allow the voice of fear to dictate how she lives her life.

A French-born Buddhist nun ordained in England in the late seventies, Ajahn Sundara teaches that we should *be with* our fear with compassion, patience and 'the tenderness of a mother with her only newborn child':

> Usually we refuse to experience fear. We try either to get rid of it or immediately resolve the situation that triggers it. So with patience, we can witness the mind running through its reactive, patterned responses to fear. And by opening to the pain those patterns cause, both the patterns and the fear itself will eventually end. Fear is so deeply embedded that we have to be clever in relating to it. It often tricks us into believing that it doesn't belong as part of our conscious experience. Then we can spend a lot of energy trying to avoid fear or keep it at bay.

Interviewed in *Inquiring Mind*, a journal for meditators, Ajahn Sundara described her experience on a retreat where she worked with her fear:

> I vowed that if fear arose, however convincing it seemed, I would not try to resolve it, 'let it go', or anything but simply be aware of it. By the end of the retreat, as the fear came and went my

heart was at peace with it. The anticipation, aversion and desire to control it had been the real causes of suffering, not the fear itself. This was when I learned the importance of patience in uncovering all the layers of the root of my fear.

Camilla and Ajahn Sundara are not the only women who make a priority of working with their fears. Betsy is a mother of two boys who is also a close friend from my Buddhist group. Managing fear is a dominating aspect of her practice, for fear has been her main teacher for some years. Bright and warm, Betsy is one of the most inspiring Buddhist mothers I know: self-aware, generous in sharing what she learns even if it means revealing her vulnerabilities to others, but most of all, tireless in her service to our Buddhist group. This is how she tells her story of fear:

For many years I worked as a counsellor at a women's refuge, listening to countless stories of violence and trauma. While in this position, one of our clients, who was mentally ill, brutally murdered another woman at the refuge and escaped with her children. The children were rescued, but the murder traumatised me and unleashed the cumulative effect of all those stories of mothers' terror.

Since then I've traversed two major breakdowns, both due to 'anxious depression'. I have known fear intimately and have listened to the scary stories in the mind that have tricked me into believing I'm weak, powerless and worthless, the hateful voices of self-blame and shame.

Still, somehow I knew that I would be okay, that there was a part of me fear could not touch. Both of the breakdowns were really breakthroughs. They were challenges to radically change the way I lived—huge wake-up calls. I loved my work and tried to carry on as before, but after the second breakdown I realised it was time to leave, that I needed to 'nourish the seeds of joy within', as Thich Nhat Hanh says.

Different fears arose in me after leaving work. I hadn't realised how much my sense of identity was caught up in being a counsellor, a helper. Who was I, if not a counsellor? My former confidence gave way to great doubts about myself and my abilities. Everything had changed. Nothing could be taken for granted. When I was very fragile I couldn't do much, but as I began to get better I needed to learn how much I could safely do without getting overwhelmed again. This required a new way of being in the world, a deep listening to that quiet voice within. And through the listening I began to stop my habitual rushing around, lost in thought, and instead could remind myself to breathe and tune in to the body, the present moment.

Eventually, I made three vows: I vow to live fearlessly. I vow to abandon worry and agitation. I vow to live with love.

These vows resonate within me in my daily life, reminding me that I have a choice. I can either buy into the scary stories the mind creates, or I can drop them and come back to the breath, the sound of the birds singing, the reflection of sunlight on water. Sometimes it's as simple as that: I can choose to react habitually with craving or aversion, or I can let go by opening up to love. Other times I need to turn towards the fear, to sit with it with open curiosity. When I'm able to do that, it loses its power to scare me. And I can discover fearlessness right in the midst of fear.

Compassion and understanding of the suffering of others grew in me. As I slowly felt my way back into the world my heart was attuned to others who were also wounded. There was healing through love and connection. It's like orientating my compass to love, not fear. As one of my teachers said, 'When we shift out of fear and anxiety, we change, and everything changes around us.'

I expect fear will continue to challenge me—possibly even overwhelming me again. What helps when the going gets rough is to remember the Buddha's wise words: 'This is not mine. This is not me. This is not my self.' There is no need to take the fear personally; it is just the natural consequence of past conditions.

I take refuge in the Buddha, his teachings and my Buddhist group. Although I'd been meditating off and on most of my adult life, meditation now became a priority. I rarely miss a day anymore.

Betsy is in good company in using meditation as one of her tools to deal with fear. The Dalai Lama used to be afraid of planes, but has conquered his fear of flying, these days using his time in the air to meditate. Betsy emphasises, however, that meditation on its own would never have been enough to help her deal with fear. Meditation is one aspect of the Buddha's path out of suffering but needs to be balanced by ethics and wisdom. For Betsy, wise friends and teachers in the Buddhist community were also essential, along with the professional help required of her condition.

I asked Betsy what it means to make a vow to live fearlessly, given that she admits fear is likely to always be with her.

For me that vow really helps. I made the vow alongside a group of people making similar vows so the ceremony formalised it for me. But most importantly, making the vow set an intention. My inner compass was set to love not fear so the vow gives me an orientation that stays with me. When I need to make a decision, such as recently deciding whether to start a new relationship with a man, fear still arises. Yet having made my vow I could observe the fear, but still make a courageous decision to commit to a relationship. My fear no longer rules my life.

One common point for all these women—Camilla, Ajahn Sundara and Betsy—is that none of them say they have conquered fear once and for all. It is likely to remain a regular visitor, but they have been able to enter into a completely different relationship with their fear—one characterised by openness, curiosity and compassion—which has significantly minimised the suffering fear brings.

One concluding tip for being with fear comes from the Venerable Thich Nhat Hanh, who advises us, when we see fear arise, to say, 'Hello fear, I know you well.' In doing this, we not only label the emotion and bring conscious awareness and a little objective distance to it, but we remind ourselves that we have survived this mind state in the past: its arrival is no cause for panic. It is just another impermanent emotion passing through the system.

WORRYING VERSUS SEEING CLEARLY

Living in a state of delusion, according to the Buddha, yet to understand the causes and conditions for our problems, nor the impermanent, unsatisfactory nature of all we cling to, few of us see our problems clearly. Sarah Edelman, author of *Change Your Thinking*, discusses the habit of worrying, providing two interesting examples of how we cling to unrealistic ways of seeing. First:

> As strange as it may seem, people sometimes unconsciously assume that worrying is protective—that it prevents our feared situation from eventuating. If in the past you have frequently worried about potential disasters that never came to pass, this may have caused you to make an unconscious association between worrying and positive outcomes.

This sounds nothing short of superstitious: somehow we believe that worrying magically increases our control of a situation. Interestingly, she describes this as an unconscious assumption. If we could only catch ourselves worrying in the mistaken belief that the very act makes us safer, we might free ourselves from quite a number of the chains of worry.

The second unrealistic belief mothers might hold about worrying, according to Edelman, is this one:

> . . . it prepares them for the worst. As one woman put it: 'If I expect some disaster, and it doesn't happen, then I will enjoy the relief. If it does happen, then at least I'll have prepared myself.'

Yet as Edelman points out, how much time has this woman spent in a state of dread and negativity in the process of preparing herself for the worst, denying herself peace of mind along the way? The worry often causes us more pain than the situation we dread.

I long ago memorised the words of the French Renaissance writer Michel de Montaigne, 'My life has been full of terrible misfortunes, most of which never happened.' He is right: the vast majority of what we worry about never comes about, and even if it does, our ability to cope is often better than we expect. That is not to say trouble never strikes. Yet, as Camilla has found, and has told me many times, her greatest lessons and spiritual breakthroughs have all come about as a direct result of suffering.

WHEN TROUBLE DOES STRIKE . . .

Sometimes, we have undeniably sound reasons to experience fear and anxiety. Our child is seriously ill, injured or unhappy. They may hate school, their teacher, or children who are persecuting or excluding them. Or our fear might come from a disaster in our own situation: our finances, our marriage, our health or the suffering of someone close to us. The potential exists for our nights to become sleepless, our bodies to fill with tension and our thoughts to circle tortuously. Yet as mothers, we cannot afford to go to pieces for we need to stay strong for our children. While we feel compassion and empathy for our children when they suffer, we cannot afford to let our feelings overwhelm us.

It helps to focus on what needs doing by asking ourselves, 'What does this moment require of me?' When we can be present to the needs of the moment, we save ourselves from becoming lost in nightmarish scenarios of the future, or regrets about past behaviour that we can no longer change. Try to be aware of your feelings as they unfold, even labelling them—'anger', 'sadness', 'anxiety'—for the very act of bringing conscious awareness to our emotions reduces their intensity and allows you the space that comes from taking a psychological step back.

Christine is a loving and devoted mother but learned how she could distort her love for her son into self-flagellation.

My son had trouble settling in to his first year of school. I think I started him at too young an age. His teacher found his high spirits frustrating and he wasn't fitting in socially either. I could see his self-confidence dropping and it was breaking my heart. I endured months of worrying and sleepless nights. In the end I withdrew him from school mid-year so that he could start afresh the following year, and in hindsight this was the right decision.

One of my regrets about this episode is the way I treated myself. At such a tough time for me I kept criticising myself over my misjudgement about his readiness for school but also for my very feelings. I kept saying to myself that I should not feel anxious or scared or stressed yet could not seem to impose a calmer, happier state on myself.

I was clinging to an image of myself as an optimist, as stoic and unflappable, but I think the battle to feel other than I felt increased the pain of the experience. If I am ever in this kind of situation again, I hope I can accept whatever emotion I experience with more compassion for myself, accepting that this is what I am feeling for now rather than trying to change it or suppress it.

No matter what is happening or how we are feeling, it is always possible to find some stillness within, for it is always there. Meditation is the most effective way to connect with this stillness: our anxious thoughts quieten, our muscles relax and inner space opens before us. The spaciousness we discover in our own minds almost magically changes our perspective on our problem and we start to re-imagine ourselves as stronger.

Of course, at times we feel too anxious to even meditate, or it might be more appropriate to take the necessary steps to solve our problem sooner rather than later. We sometimes lack time to meditate when crises strike. Yet even a brief pause, where we momentarily return to our bodies, attune to our breathing and inhabit the moment, will ground us and equip us to cope more courageously and from a wiser place within us.

EXPECTATIONS INFORMED BY FEAR

Heather is a Buddhist mother who was able to notice the fear underlying her expectations of her daughter.

I grew up in a time of quite high unemployment. When it came time for me to look for a job I had trouble landing one. I wanted to work in advertising but there was so much competition that it was nearly impossible for a new graduate to find work. Without a fallback plan, I spent several years doing jobs I did not enjoy before eventually retraining as a teacher. Now, as a mother, these experiences have affected the way I parent. It has only been half-conscious, but I think I have been obsessed with raising children who will be 'employable'. For a while, this meant I was quite hard on my first-born. I have painful memories of yelling at her and losing my patience when I perceived her to be too slow at learning to count, to read, or to understand new concepts.

I would actually lose my temper with her when she struggled with something and then feel really ashamed of myself. Eventually I could see that my reaction was not a simple matter of impatience but also one of fear. It was as though I was yelling: *You must prove to me that you are clever, otherwise I have to face my fear that you will never have a satisfying career!* I expected my daughter to put my mind at ease. I didn't want to worry about her experiencing my frustration in the workforce, and I assumed the best insurance was for her to be a quick learner and a high achiever.

Seeing the fear in my reactions helped me to stop reacting so negatively. These days I make an effort to notice the fear arise, acknowledge it, and return to what the present moment requires. My fears about the distant future had been blinding me to the needs of the present. In the present moment my daughter might need help with what she is learning, and if I do it with patience and compassion my help is more effective and allows her self-confidence to grow.

Many of us have the habit of projecting our children into the future, training them for adulthood, rather than meeting them as the child they are right now. I know my impatience with my sons as we prepare to leave the house reaches a peak when I taunt myself, 'How will they ever survive in the workforce when they can't even master the daily clothes-shoes-teeth routine?'

In her excellent book *Choosing Happiness*, Stephanie Dowrick describes the role of fear and anxiety when we torment our children with our expectations:

> Fear and anxiety drive this phenomenon: fear that there are not enough of the good things to go around; anxiety that you will 'miss out' not just on the good things but on the love, approval and applause that seem to go with them. So enslaved are many of us by these fears of insufficiency that they drive our behavior even towards our youngest children.
>
> We want our children to be 'ahead' before they are even standing.
>
> We compare our children's progress using measures more suitable for the workplace than the classroom.
>
> We require our children to sacrifice pleasure, creativity, spontaneity and even co-operation and social rewards because of our concerns about their eventual status and income. (And concerns about how their choices reflect on us.)

She speaks of the tendency to support their choices—of subjects to study and potential careers—only when they ensure our children will be competitive in the economy, ignoring concerns about whether they will be 'well-rounded, fully alive human beings' who have followed their true interests and aspirations.

A common question at Buddhist meetings is, 'How can you practise non-attachment with your own children?' How would you even define it? The answer lies in allowing our children their autonomy, the freedom to be who they are, free from the hopes, fears and aspirations of their parents. With each passing year, we need to practise letting go of more control and allowing them more freedom to be who they are. Children never grow into replicas of their parents just as they never grow up to fulfil our precise dreams of who they will be. Non-attachment is about letting go of limiting expectations and loving our children as they are.

Yesterday on the radio I listened to a program about relationship breakdowns between parents and their grown children. It was heartbreaking to hear the various young adults calling in, voices trembling with pain, describing why they could not enjoy a fully loving relationship with their parents: two callers were gay; one caller had a very religious mother who never forgave her three daughters after they all became pregnant as teenagers; one man struggled with a workaholic father who could not accept his son's need to regularly go out and enjoy himself with friends. One young Christian woman rang heartbroken by her parents' highly vocal rejection of her faith over the last eight years. Almost all of them expressed deep disappointment that their parents could not accept them for who they are. All wanted to be loved unconditionally. Their stories were tragic examples of how attachment to our views—about sexuality, religion, morality—cause suffering.

CHILDHOOD FEARS

It is normal and common, as most of us have witnessed, for children of any age to harbour what strikes us as irrational fears. One day, lolling around our local library, Zac displayed an interest in aliens and UFOs. Always keen to indulge a new interest as a means to make Zac read more, I collected a large pile of books on this new topic and Zac took them home and devoured them in one sitting. That was eighteen months ago, and ever since he has been afraid of being alone in case he is abducted by aliens.

Zac has expressed shame over his feelings of fear, believing that he should be braver at his age. Yet there is no point trying to suppress fear or trying to 'snap out of it'. That would only be denial, which could never solve the problem. As I have tried to teach Zac, it is possible to be both fearful and courageous at the same time, for what is courage if not acting in spite of our feelings of fear. Without fear, what is to overcome? It has helped to explain to him that fear is a natural part of childhood for the great majority of children, each new fear being a phase that children eventually work through.

A sense of lacking control is the source of fear, so it helps to provide information to increase our child's sense of control—for example, according to Wikipedia there is no scientific evidence of alien abductions. Zac has also been interested to learn that fear has evolutionary causes: throughout the millennia children have faced all manner of dangers, from wild animals to violent conflicts, and the ability to feel fear has produced the physiological reactions—the increased heart rate, the heightened sensory alertness, the bodily tension—to help them cope with a crisis. With fear, their bodies were ready for flight or fight.

•

You may have seen statues of the Buddha where he has his right arm raised, palm facing forward. Although a Westerner might interpret this as meaning 'stop', it in fact means, 'do not fear', and was, according to legend, the gesture the Buddha made immediately on achieving enlightenment. The Buddha used this gesture again to subdue, successfully, the rampaging elephant that his jealous cousin Devadatta once set loose on him. Observing and becoming familiar with the patterns of our fear is central to Buddhist practice, fear being at the core of all our cravings.

When the Buddha taught about generosity, he taught that there are four things we can give: spiritual guidance, protection from danger, material aid and fearlessness. With the 'do not fear' hand gesture the Buddha bestows fearlessness on us and teaches that we can do the same to others. By cultivating fearlessness in ourselves, through meditation and other practices that deepen our awareness, we can share fearlessness with others through our example. Striving for relatively fearless parenting, for example, we are perhaps more likely to raise children free from excessive anxiety and worry.

Inquiry

- Have you found a healthy point of balance between over-protectiveness and abandon when it comes to creating safe boundaries for your children?
- Do your children ever practise dealing with discomfort or difficulty?
- Do you insist that life conform to your plans and preferences or can you practise equanimity—a degree of acceptance of whatever happens?
- Do you ever question your 'needs'? Do you really need so much of whatever it is you pursue? How often do you switch to noticing the abundance of what you already have?
- Would you consider making a vow to live fearlessly?
- When fear arises do you meet it with compassion and patience? Could you pause and 'be with it' rather than react habitually?
- Do you, at some level, believe your worrying protects you from what you fear?

- Do you ever consider the stillness and space meditation provides as a way to counteract fear or anxiety?
- In times of crisis, can you be kind to yourself? Can you label—and accept—the various emotions that arise? Can you bring yourself to say, *This too will pass*?
- Do you ever *pause* and reconnect to the stillness that is always within you?
- Do you treat your children as children with a right to a childhood or as trainee adults?
- Are you aware of the effects of your expectations on your children? Do you need them to become certain types of people?
- Can you be patient and understanding about your children's seemingly irrational fears?

CHAPTER 8

self

WITH CHILDREN AT SCHOOL our roles as mothers shift and we feel ourselves to be a different kind of 'self' as we wonder, 'Who am I now?' To answer this question we rely on our new role as a mother of schoolchildren—who wears the hats of taxi-driver, homework assistant, social consultant, life coach and volunteer—to define a new self. This all sounds harmless enough. Yet to see ourselves in terms of a temporary role is limiting and unrealistic, for we are so much more.

Relying on a role to define ourselves is a symptom of a sense of not being enough as we are. Our role serves our insatiable need for a sense of a consistent self yet is no reliable source of lasting happiness because no roles last forever. Over-identifying with our role as a mother can lead to extreme behaviours such as over-protectiveness, over-attentiveness, expecting too much from our children, doing their homework for them, or rescuing them too often rather than letting them learn to take responsibility and grow into autonomous beings.

Just as Betsy decribed in the last chapter, Camilla also makes a practice of chanting the words of the Buddha throughout her day, 'This is not mine, this is not what I am, this is not my self.' In this way, she avoids mistaking her role as a mother—or her role as an accountant, or anything else she owns, thinks or does—for who she is. She is already who she is, regardless of what part she plays in a house, school or workplace.

Stories of spiritual awakening—whether they come from non-Buddhists such as the writer Eckhart Tolle, great Buddhist masters, or ordinary individuals—seem to have one point in common. These transcendent moments revolve around an insight into selflessness, egolessness, or a halt in our habitual sense of separation from the world and others. Even mainstream culture has detected this common characteristic: in *The Simpsons Movie* Homer experiences a spiritual awakening under the guidance of an American Indian woman. The moment was only possible when he saw the obstacle of self-centredness, after which his whole body separates into its parts which float in all directions and then reassemble anew. His 'self', we are to believe, needed to dissipate before any insight was possible. As in the case of Homer, these blissful transformations, which change one's whole perception of reality, are not likely to last long for most who experience them (but more about that in the final chapter).

A BUSLOAD OF SELVES

Part of understanding that we are not a fixed, unchanging, consistent self is to acknowledge that our mind presents numerous different selves who all jostle for our attention. Our minds are effectively a whole busload of selves, such that the question at any point in time is not so much 'Who am I?' as 'Who is currently driving the bus?' None of the selves we observe are 'who we are' for none of them has a permanent position in the driver's seat.

I have found it useful to identify and name some of the selves that drop in more regularly. That way I can greet them by name and be open and curious about the form they might take today. Labelling them as they appear, I am less likely to take them seriously or let them push me around. I start to see some of them as a bit of a joke, declaring, *Oh, you again!* There is no need to silence or eliminate even the more trouble-making selves. A Buddhist learns to watch them all and be open, curious and tolerant.

I have compiled a list over the page of some of the selves that sometimes drive my bus. It may appear self-indulgent putting readers through a dissection of my personality, yet if belonging to a Buddhist community has squashed one delusion in me, it is that I am some kind of 'special case'. I have learned over the years, with great relief, that my mind states, stories and inner dramas are, to varying degrees, common to everyone. To take any of these as evidence that I am a self, completely separate from others, is delusional. Just to be sure that I was not exposing any unique neuroses I asked a couple of my Buddhist friends to tell me if there were any 'selves' in my list that had never visited them—and there were not. Identifying our less skilful selves helps us feel compassion for others as we come to realise that everyone plays host to similar visitors.

My list seems to focus on my more negative selves—the stirrers—such that I might sound overly critical. Yet the point of noticing and labelling these 'characters' is to remind ourselves we needn't identify with them or see them as 'who I am'. They are all impermanent. I, like you, also have Buddha Nature giving rise to selves I might name 'Compassionate Self' or 'Wise Self'. The Buddha does want us to notice these wiser selves. This was his Third Noble Truth: 'suffering can end, so realise it.' In other words, pause and notice the times you have let go of craving and behaved skilfully. Come to know what that feels like. See these 'higher' selves clearly and they are more likely to visit again.

So, introducing some of my selves:

Sneering Bloke Self

I first noticed this self while having some dark moments on a retreat. This is the self that uses bad language and rolls his eyes in derision. He is cynical and likely to see others as morons. Everything is a joke to him, especially Buddhists. Alcohol can bring him out into the light of day. I imagine that if the seeds of this self were watered sufficiently, this is the part of me that might be capable of committing atrocities in times of war. Why is this self a male? Probably because he reminds me of many boys I grew up with who might have been using a sneering bloke facade as a way to look cool and tough.

I could always feel really, really guilty whenever Sneering Bloke Self turns up or I could try to kill him on sight, but the Buddhist approach is to merely keep an eye on him so I always know what he's up to. He will leave when he is ready.

Clipboard Self

This is the self who constantly evaluates my performance. Whether I am playing sport, singing, socialising or working, she stands by with her clipboard ticking check boxes and assessing how good I am. Her dominance can undermine any joy I might find in daily activities so she is worth noticing and learning about. Clipboard Self is also running a collection agency, desperately collating feedback on how I have performed, sometimes focusing solely on all the positive feedback, other times trying to come to terms with any criticism. Sometimes her feedback comes from comparing herself with others on any number of indicators, but usually she uses her own standards no matter how unrealistic they are.

Inadequate Self

If Clipboard Self spends too much time on negative feedback, she might suddenly change into Inadequate Self, who tends to start her sentences with the words: *I'm no good at . . .*, *I wish I was more . . .*, *I'm always stuffing up . . .*, *Oh no, my third mistake!*, *Why am I the only one incapable of . . . ?* Of all the selves, she is the one who can create the most sadness.

Alienated Self

This self feels cut off from others, probably the result of focusing on perceived differences. This self says things like: *I have nothing in common with these people, I just don't fit in, I don't belong.* Alienated Self might drop in after I have suffered an awkward social occasion or an unsatisfying conversation. She has a heightened sense of her own isolation, sometimes feeling lonely and disconnected. She reminds herself that nobody else feels this way, only her, for she is a 'special case'.

Drama Queen Self

This self exaggerates the importance of insignificant events. Madly adding stories and deeper meanings, this is the self that sees off-the-cuff remarks from others as deliberate insults. Fights with her husband can only lead to divorce. Colds lead to pneumonia and then death. A bad day is the beginning of the end. Criticism, or any form of social rejection, feels like a near-death experience. Drama Queen believes she can read the minds of others as well as predict the future.

Bored Self

She talks like this: *Something is lacking in my life. I need excitement. Every day is the same. God, I hate housework. What have I got to look forward to?* She is forever checking her emails in case any interesting news has arrived that could liven up her present moment. She feels restless.

I'll-Be-Happy-When Self

This self postpones happiness until a certain desire has been achieved: *I'll be happy when I find the right job, I'll be happy when this renovation is finished, I'll be happy when my children learn to listen, I'll be happy when my husband understands me better.* She often feels resentful about the sheer length of a process: *It should have happened by now!*

This self could also be called Not-Enough Self. *Whatever I have is not enough. I must get more. Whoever I am is not enough. I must improve. Whoever other people are is not enough. They need to lift their game.* This self sees only lack and insufficiency so cannot be happy until some future point in time—that never comes. She approaches her letterbox full of hope and feels disappointed to find only bills. She picks up the ringing phone only to feel frustrated with who has decided to call her.

Comparing Self

This character compulsively compares herself with those around her so that she can decide whether she is inferior or superior. She may focus on physical beauty, wealth, intelligence, career success, parenting skills, self-confidence, social skills or whatever theme is dominating her mind. She may use her children as objects to compare with other children. She is a close relation to Clipboard Self, who is always assessing her performance. She is blind to the fact that comparing ourselves to others is just one more way to keep our false, constructed sense of self alive, and ensures our separateness from others.

•

Each of these selves seem to be visitors dropping in for a while before eventually leaving and making way for the next visitor. A much-loved poem in many a Buddhist circle is 'The Guesthouse', written by the prolific Sufi poet Rumi.

> This being human is a guest house.
> Every morning a new arrival.
>
> A joy, a depression, a meanness,
> some momentary awareness comes
> as an unexpected visitor.
>
> Welcome and entertain them all!
> Even if they are a crowd of sorrows,
> who violently sweep your house
> empty of its furniture,
> still, treat each guest honorably.
> He may be clearing you out
> for some new delight.
>
> The dark thought, the shame, the malice,
> meet them at the door laughing
> and invite them in.
>
> Be grateful for whatever comes,
> because each has been sent
> as a guide from beyond.

Who is driving the bus? Who is visiting the guesthouse? Forgive me for mixing metaphors, but it is worth being aware of our inner committee of selves and closely observing any that seek to dominate the meeting.

YOU ARE ALREADY COMPLETE

When it comes to the psychology of the 'self', Buddhist philosophy teaches the opposite to modern Western thinking. The self-help industry, the psychotherapy tradition and the culture of consumption give us the relentless message that we are not enough the way we are. We need to improve, expand and enhance our strengths and eradicate our flaws. We feel the need to build a strong ego, capable of withstanding any assault, yet the more time we spend building this ego, the more fragile it feels.

We seek reassurance from self-esteem, self-development, self-control, self-realisation, yet imagine if we could let go of all these constructs from time to time and experiment with feeling whole just as we are, right now, unconditionally. How often do we surrender to emptying our minds instead of perpetually cramming new knowledge and experiences into them? Would stopping the flow of thoughts for a few moments make us any less ourselves?

In *Opening the Lotus: A Woman's Guide to Buddhism* Sandy Boucher writes about her reaction when an inspiring teacher from Germany, who had resolved her own traumas following wartime suffering, tells her, 'There is nothing that can be added to you, and nothing can be taken away.' Sandy was moved by a strong sense that the teacher had realised this truth for herself on a deep level for she radiated a 'deep serenity, a *sureness*'. Sandy writes:

> I felt a relaxation in myself, as if I had been shown the end of striving, of struggling, of trying. Why struggle when we are

already, each of us, a part of the essential nature of the universe? Awareness of this deep harmony can provide us with much more real strength and stability than reliance on our usual limited, ever shifting selves.

In the West we have so come to value self-esteem, in ourselves and in our children, that we feel shocked and confused by Buddhist teachings about the need to see our sense of self as a convenient fabrication. Do we not need some belief in ourselves in order to function? Is a stable self-esteem not crucial to finding any happiness in life? Aren't people with no sense of self-worth just as vulnerable as those with over-inflated egos? After all, didn't we always feel depressed at the times when we felt we were failing to measure up? And isn't self-confidence one of the qualities we most want for our children?

We do need a sense of self in order to play our role in society and feel some stability as a person. Children whose sense of self was never allowed to develop normally grew into the most troubled adults. Our problem lies in exaggerating the reality of the self. As a result, we isolate ourselves from others and deny ourselves a more expansive, inclusive relationship with all that surrounds us. Too engaged by the considerable needs of ego-maintenance, we fail to connect with the world outside our own skin. Clinging to our sense of self, we cannot see clearly for the illusion of an independent, separate self, in complete control of its own behaviour, inevitably distorts our vision. We see people, objects and our surroundings only in terms of our own self-interest.

AWARENESS—BUT WITH COMPASSION

Many mothers write web logs, or blogs, on the internet where they regularly record their musings on their experience of motherhood. In one such blog called *Mama's So Mindful*, mother of two Rachel

Springfield writes with striking honesty and insight. She understands that the line between self and other is far more blurred than we usually assume:

> Carl Jung said if there is anything you would want to change in a child, examine it and see if it is not something that would be better changed in yourself. I say this is true for all people, not just children. When I take the time to notice, I see how some of the most irritating behaviours in others are ones that I share with them. Or ones that I am even worse at! It is not easy to step back and reflect. It hurts. Seeing things you don't like about yourself is not fun. But it makes me a better person every time I walk through the process.
>
> So here are some ugly things I see in myself. Hold the mirror steady, here I go.
>
> I often feel angry about how others aren't supportive of me and my family because they are too self-involved. Put that one on paper and it gets pretty obvious who is self-involved, eh?
>
> My son's controlling behaviour sometimes gets on my nerves. I mean, when he doesn't play MY WAY that's controlling, right? Hmmm.
>
> I often feel unloved. The more I obsess about it, the more I look for evidence that people love me and the more they fail at showing me. In the meantime, what am I doing but withholding my own love based on my judgments? Ouch. That one stings.
>
> I want others to be more patient, more kind, more relaxed in the pressured times. I can't be, so why would I even think of expecting that of someone else?

A Buddhist teacher would argue that through Rachel's awareness of her own behaviour she is at least halfway towards enacting more skilful responses in the future. Yet although Rachel excels in taking responsibility for her own tendencies, there is an element of stern self-judgement in there as she refers to 'ugly things I see in myself'. I suspect any Buddhist teacher would tell her to attempt some compassion as she observes her behaviour. In Buddhist practice, awareness is supposed to be non-judgemental.

Besides, the tendencies she writes about are not *who she is*. They are simply phenomena arising in response to numerous conditions, some under her control, many not. Since we are not usually mindful, we cannot claim there is a self inside us controlling or choosing our behaviour—we can only respond to conditions, or enact our karma. None of our states of mind can represent who we are, given that our mind goes through numerous states in a single day and may include everything from joyful optimism to world-hating despair. Her habitual responses are by no means unique to her, since we all struggle with hindrances such as anger, greed and worry—they are part of the human condition and no basis on which to construct a self that is separate from others.

As Buddhist teacher and comedian from the States Wes Nisker puts it: *You are not your fault!* This, of course, raises the question of responsibility: if my actions are not my fault, then I am no longer responsible for them. Wes replies that we can indeed take responsibility, but only for what we are aware of. How could we ever change something we cannot even see? The more clearly we see the causes, conditions and consequences of our behaviour, the more likely we are to manage what we think, say and do.

If we wanted to change our behaviour, rather than wishing we were different or berating ourselves, we would need to do something about the conditions supporting our actions. For example, if we wanted to stop being critical and mean-spirited towards others, we could regularly practise lovingkindness meditation where we genuinely wish others well, thereby replacing malevolent thoughts with benevolent ones. If we wanted to be less angry, we could make a study of our anger in order to understand what it is we cling to. If we wanted to be less controlling we might investigate what it is we fear. Understanding can be the crucial condition that paves the way to change, or, in Buddhist terms, liberation from suffering.

A couple of weeks later, Rachel addressed the issue of compassion for herself in her blog:

Compassion? What's that again? Oh you mean that thing I give to OTHER people . . .

I am a loving, generous person who generally believes the best of people, who generally believes that people are doing the best they can at that moment, and who commits utterly to the concept that we are here on the planet to grow, learn, experience, and evolve.

Unless it's me. I am just . . . failing to meet the minimum standard, which apparently for me, means perfect. Hmmm. Even when I am consciously trying to increase my level of self-kindness, I get busted for the self-deprecating or downright mean ways I talk (and think) about myself.

I was just talking to a friend about being more compassionate and called myself a DORK in the same sentence. And I didn't notice. She pointed it out, kindly and gently. This time I laughed. Other times, I would then use that 'error' to beat myself up even more.

Sometimes I almost get it. The golden ring is at my fingertips. I notice myself being really kind to me, and notice it extending to being even more compassionate to others. Especially my son. Especially when he is pushing my buttons. By being four.

SENSE OF SELF IN CHILDREN

The Buddha taught that our need to construct and maintain our false view of a consistent, separate self was a primary cause of our general inability to be happy. Have we not all witnessed for ourselves the extreme cases—those whose lives are completely driven by their ego-needs, those who are blind to any aspect of life that does not cater directly to their ego? Completely dependent on external circumstances—such as positive feedback and popularity—any happiness they find is vulnerable. We only have to read some celebrity gossip to find evidence of how slaving in the service of a hungry ego—be it through seeking fame, wealth or a sense of one's own specialness—tends to end somewhere like rehab.

Many social commentators have observed the need in modern parents to teach their children that they are 'special'. I can almost picture the Buddha shaking his head: this is not the path to happiness. In her book *Consuming Innocence*, Karen Brooks laments the effects of popular culture on our children, reserving a chapter to attack our need to raise 'little princesses'. She opens the chapter remarking on how the word 'ordinary' has evolved into an insult, asking: 'When did being "ordinary" become a synonym for loser?' She also raises the logical question, how can we *all* be special?

In concluding the chapter she writes: 'The truth is most of our kids are going to be, in the great scheme of things, ordinary . . . There's nothing wrong with ordinary, particularly if it also implies well-balanced, content and comfortable in their own skin.'

Even though her book goes nowhere near Buddhist teachings, the final sentences of the chapter acknowledge how the need to feel like a 'special' self only increases a sense of separation from others:

By focusing on the individual and what makes us 'special', we create an 'us' and 'them' mentality. Instead of looking for what makes us the same, ideologically, morally and ethically, we search for that which distinguishes us as different. We exaggerate the little things (often superficial or external only) to make them count and miss that which we can delight in sharing—with each other and our children. And in doing so we forget that without 'we', there's no community.

From what I have read over the years about the dangers of overinflating a child's self-esteem, I have learned to be moderate with praise, to reserve it for occasions when it is genuinely due, to be specific about what they have done well and to be sensitive but honest about what needs more work. We want our children to enjoy their activities rather than perform them only for the reward of praise. In trying to practise this middle-ground approach, I have felt challenged by the current environment where my boys constantly bring home 'awards' from school. I have witnessed long assemblies, in a normal school week, where at least a quarter of the school population collect a certificate. I have witnessed young soccer players win trophies for coming last in the competition. What is left to work for anymore when absolutely everybody is so special? Praise these days is so cheap. How many children are we setting up for one mighty great fall later in life when they realise they are not so invincible?

Or maybe I am indulging in a rant. The Buddha taught that being attached to any view—and the one I expressed in the last paragraph would be no exception—will cause me to suffer. Besides, the issue of praise is far from clear-cut. As I coach the struggling readers at school for an hour each week I am told to praise what they get right and to make a fuss over any improvements. Sometimes I witness immense relief in the eyes of such children to hear some praise, as though they really need the encouragement to help them along through a challenging, and sometimes even humiliating, process.

How much to praise children—finding a middle ground—is definitely a tricky business that we should probably avoid generalising about. Since every child is different, it is best left to our mother's intuition of what is best in the long run for our children. Mother's intuition, of course, works best when we have been mindful and conscious throughout our day rather than flying on automatic pilot. The challenge is to see the big picture, the causes and conditions we set up for our children, as clearly as possible. We need to provide the necessary encouragement and support, without raising children who have come to depend on constant praise, who lose their capacity to act for the sheer intrinsic enjoyment of an activity.

An almost forgotten and definitely unfashionable virtue in our age, preoccupied as it is with developing self-esteem, is humility. It is a value we all admire when we see it, yet how often do we think to nurture it in our offspring? While we will find no lack of books on how to develop confident children, we will not find any on developing humility. Believe me, when Alex was around four years old I diligently searched for one. The act of developing humility arguably has a bad reputation, reminding us of the parents of yore who never praised their children in case they gave them a 'big head'. Or we think of those repressive, religious families who sought to raise God-fearing, self-denying children. Daughters throughout history have been raised to be humble, self-effacing and self-sacrificing.

Yet there is a wiser form of humility that we ascribe to the truly great, such as Nelson Mandela, the Dalai Lama, Mahatma Gandhi, Burma's Aung San Suu Kyi and Arundhati Roy, the Indian author and human-rights campaigner. Humility is the opposite of self-obsession, the narcissism which so detracts from our chances for long-term contentment. Humility, as opposed to excessive pride in yourself, is a more realistic way to be in the world as it recognises the vastness of what we do not know, the enormity of our debt of gratitude to others, and the certainty of our eventual demise and death. Excessive pride in ourselves can only lead to a fall, whereas humility drastically reduces our vulnerability in the world for we have far less to lose. Humility is helpful in interpersonal relationships: the humble never snub others but rather open their hearts to whoever they meet.

We live in a time where most of us are overly concerned with what image we project to others, but is this a way of being in the world that will bring us contentment? Do we want to teach our children to prioritise their public image and physical appearance, to see themselves as the centre of the universe, to need constant affirmation from others? Nurturing humility in our children is about teaching them openness to the needs and suffering of others, and awareness of our interconnectedness and dependence on others. While praising them for their achievements, we can also acknowledge the role of those who helped them achieve any impressive results—such as their teacher, members of the school community or other inspiring figures.

PROTECTING OUR CHILDREN FROM A FALSE 'SELF'

When we give our children the message that our love is conditional on their meeting our expectations, we cultivate in them a false self. In his book *The Gifts of Parenting*, Italian Buddhist father Piero Ferrucci, an eminent psychologist, bravely shares the lingering effects of his mother's expectations.

> All my mother's expectations have weighed on me, however much she loved me. Even now, after so many years, I sometimes have

the feeling I am living an existence that is not entirely mine, a life whose course has been decided by someone else. If I have an ambition, for example, I am not sure it is really mine. Maybe I am trying to satisfy the need of someone who is no longer here, but whose expectations live on in me. And I risk doing the same to [my son] Emilio. Understanding this lesson is a long way from assimilating it, however. In the school of life I am a slow student, and I have to tackle the same lesson many times.

Rather than turning inward when they make their choices in life, many children develop the habit of choosing actions that bring them love and acceptance. They become dependent on praise, approval and social acceptance. Always second-guessing what others want them to be, they risk losing touch with their own inner voice. Without regular opportunities to make their own choices based on what feels right for them, they risk losing the self-confidence to make their own decisions. Unconditional love from parents creates space for the growth of an individual.

It is easy to shower love on our children when they behave well, bringing home strong academic results and winning accolades. How effortlessly our love can flow at such times. Yet on the occasions when they battle with us, underachieve or lack motivation, they need to feel loved just as much, if not more. Our children need to know we love them for who they are and not how we expect them to be. This means never saying, 'I really love you when you . . .'

This is a potentially confusing area. If they have been rude to us, or lazy at school, we cannot be seen to reward them with affection. If my sons have an 'off-day' marked by mistakes, disappointments or family conflict, I make a point of tucking them into bed that night with words like, 'Even though you severely bruised your brother, I still love you.' Of course, the violence itself would have been addressed earlier. The important point is that they know they cannot do anything to diminish my affection for them. One day they will stop punching each other because they know in themselves that it is wrong, rather than as a way to safeguard their mother's love for them.

MOTHER OF X CHILDREN

We often describe mothers, as I have throughout this book, in terms of how many children they have and of what gender: 'Celia, a mother of three', 'Jenny, a mother of two girls'. Nothing contributes to our sense of identity as much as motherhood. Some women who are unable to conceive a child can feel like their life is over: without a baby they feel as though they are nobody.

In some cases a period of reflection that comes when our children start school leads mothers to pine for another child. Then again this could happen even earlier in a mother's journey, as it did for Rachel Springfield, who expresses the yearning in her blog *Mama's So Mindful*:

> I woke up again this morning missing the child that will not be. Our third child that I never really thought we would have, but somehow now want so desperately. This phantom baby syndrome came with the birth of my daughter, now almost five months old. In her early months I would literally cry while holding her and nursing, immersed in the sadness that this would be my last. My last baby to nurse, to have fall asleep on my chest, to see that first smile . . . they are small for such a short time! I am still sad about it, but it is a dull ache rather than a sharp pain.

Many a mother understands what Rachel is talking about. I know *I* do. I passionately love having two boys but often I feel a daughter-shaped hole in my life as I realise I will never know what it is like to raise a girl; I will never experience the joys of the mother–daughter relationship and all that it might have taught me. Having watched over two wailing babies, and my gruelling second pregnancy featuring nausea, diabetes and unrelenting exhaustion, my long-suffering husband decided to take matters into his own hands and took the necessary measures to ensure we would never be parents of three.

I have to concede he probably made the right decision for our family—not that this stops the pangs of yearning from visiting. While for me such feelings are a bittersweet melancholy, for many of the women around me the need for that additional child is a longing they are willing to endure anything to fulfil. Some suffer the emotional devastation of a series of miscarriages, others the trials of in-vitro fertilisation. Some lose their babies soon after birth and experience a grief beyond expression.

When a dear friend lost her newborn baby, she did not take phone calls, so I emailed her. I sent her a quote from Anne Deveson's book *Resilience*. Anne had lost an adult child but her words might apply for any mother who loses a baby.

For me, over the years, the pain of Jonathan's death has retreated and settled somewhere deep inside. I almost forget it is there. Then something will jolt my memory and the pain returns. Unexpectedly and savagely—as if this unbelievable thing that happened all those years ago needs to remind me sharply of its presence. Sometimes it comes more softly, like a cloud of gentle melancholia. The pain subsides. The cloud floats away.

Her words beautifully capture the Buddha's teaching of imperma-nence: however we feel in the present moment, the feeling will shift, fade, intensify and transform over time.

•

A new puppy in our household, a female, has filled a significant portion of the daughter-sized hole in my life. Now, I know it would be ridiculous to suggest a pet could ever take the place of a baby but I am definitely taken aback by the intensity of my love for her. I seem to be part of a wider trend: my friend Viv remarked on how the mothers at the school gate all seem to have either a new baby or a new puppy.

It is lovely to have another girl in the house. Together we form a united front against those other three brutes.

Inquiry

- Are you aware of the risks of over-identifying with your role as a mother of schoolchildren, such as the risks of curtailing your children's ability to look after themselves?
- Are you aware that nothing you do, no role you play, provides a definition of who you truly are?
- Have you been able to observe a whole busload of selves within you?
- Have you tried labelling some of the 'selves' that visit you the most often in an attempt to create some distance from which you can observe your visitor?
- Do you become caught in the mindset of our culture that we need to improve the self, and add things to it, rather than recognising your fundamental wholeness right now?

- Can you see, in your own experience, the way an exaggerated sense of self separates you from others and distorts your vision?
- Do you treat yourself with compassion as you observe your less skilful tendencies or do you take them all personally and become impatient?
- Are you raising children to believe they are 'special', or that they are part of an interdependent community?
- Are you mindful about how much you praise your children? Is the balance right?
- Do you foster in your child humility as well as self-confidence by keeping them aware of how much more we all have to learn and how much gratitude we owe to others?
- Are you teaching your children to make their own choices and solve their own problems or are they overly motivated by seeking approval from others?
- Being a mother is a major source of identity, but can you remember that you are still more than this?

CHAPTER 9

disciplining

SORRY TO USE THE word 'disciplining', which calls to mind authoritarian-style parenting with all its shaming, punishing and controlling. While we may not see ourselves as disciplinarians, we do seek to raise children with a degree of impulse-control, children who consider the needs of others—if only because it will ensure they attract love and respect, and end up happier than the selfish misfit. I use the word 'disciplining' to capture our aspiration to raise considerate children capable of a modicum of self-control (and because I have to be consistent with my one-word chapter headings!).

This is the chapter where we consider the most traditional bugbears children inflict on their mothers, such as temper outbursts, nagging, whining and self-doubt. The Buddha categorised all such behaviours under five headings, which I explore in this chapter. Of course, the Buddha was not in the business of generating detailed strategies for frazzled parents, and with so many books on the market that do so, this chapter will not enter such terrain. Yet the Buddha's insights into troublesome states of mind can help us to respond to our children's misdemeanours less automatically and more thoughtfully.

THE FIVE HINDRANCES

Many approach the practice of Buddhist teachings believing they need to change themselves, in the same way many approach parenting believing they need to change their children. Yet the Buddha taught that we already have a clear, wise mind, for that is its natural state. Rather than changing the nature of our minds, the task is to remove the obstacles, the layers of delusion that impede the natural clarity. The Buddha referred to these obstacles as the Five Hindrances, describing them as 'imperfections that defile the mind and weaken understanding'. During meditation, which is the laboratory for investigating how the mind habitually works, we have an opportunity to observe, non-judgementally, exactly what obstructs our natural clarity and we inevitably discover one, or more, of the Five Hindrances. The Buddha taught that the absence of all Five Hindrances, in any moment, is a state of pure contentment.

When our mind is in its natural state of clarity, the Buddha likened it to a pot of clear water such that you can see your face reflected. This analogy would have been especially meaningful in the time of the Buddha, when there were no mirrors, so people only knew what they looked like by seeing their reflection in water. He uses this analogy to demonstrate the effect of each hindrance on our minds.

Sense desire

'The water is mixed with red, yellow, blue or orange colour.'
Sometimes called greed, this hindrance is about craving for sensory pleasures. Our children nag for treats, sweets and television, while their mothers want chocolate, consumer goods and satisfying sex. There is nothing wrong with any of these desires in themselves, but problems arise in our obsessive attitude towards such objects, the state of mind that stops us from seeing the object of our desire clearly, for what it truly is—or more correctly, is *not*.

Ill will

'The water is seething and boiling.'
Usually referred to as anger, this hindrance relates to feelings of malice or frustration towards others or even towards objects (the broken-down car, the slow computer). It includes the full spectrum of anger, from mild irritation to raging fury.

Sloth and torpor

'The water is covered with moss and water plants.'
Sleepiness, dullness, boredom, lethargy, disengagement, apathy—this is the third hindrance.

Anxiety and worry

'The water is stirred by the wind, agitated, swaying and producing waves.'
This hindrance also includes feelings of restlessness and guilt, or any occasion when our minds are seething with so many thoughts that we cannot settle and be calm. Often called 'monkey mind', it is the mind incapable of settling into the present moment.

Doubt

'The water is stirred up and muddy.'
Described in Buddhist scriptures as 'a state of wavering and vacillation', doubt is an inability to decide or to commit. Meditators notice doubt when they hear themselves say: *What is this sitting really achieving? Why am I doing this when there are so many other things to do? I don't have what it takes anyway.* In daily life doubt manifests as *self*-doubt, self-blame, half-heartedness, indecision and confusion.

•

The hindrances cloud our judgement. In the grip of a hindrance, lost in unhelpful thoughts or fantasies, our ability to live with conscious awareness of the present moment diminishes. Not that any of the hindrances are necessarily sins, or morally wrong, for the problem lies not in the hindrance itself—which are all natural phenomena of the mind—but in our clinging to the hindrances, our tendency to become stuck, fixated and unable to see clearly.

Importantly, we need not take the hindrances personally for each of them are universal to the human condition. An angry thought, for example, was simply the arising and passing of a common phenomenon of the mind. There is no need to identify with the thought and use it to define ourselves. The anger is just one more cloud passing through the sky of our awareness. There is no point in judging, let alone punishing, ourselves. Neither do we adopt an aggressive approach where we suppress, block, or deny our experience.

On seeing a hindrance arise, we simply accept its presence and commit to seeing it more clearly. Once we see deeply and clearly how a hindrance leads to our suffering it is only natural to drop it. The importance of acceptance cannot be overstated in this process. How can we investigate an experience if we push it away? How can we investigate a hindrance if our reaction causes us to add more hindrances, making our minds too messy and complex, such as when we feel angry about feeling sleepy or when we feel anxious about feeling angry. Accepting a hindrance does not mean we act it out, only that we surrender to its presence, relax into it with keen awareness and also notice how that very approach makes the hindrance transform or fade.

Of course, the stronger our experience of a hindrance, the more important it is to investigate it. This will not necessarily come naturally for our reflex is to push a hindrance away. That's why we practise concentration, and why it is a factor of the Buddha's Eightfold Path: without it we flee at the first sign of unpleasantness. Yet pushing a hindrance away only makes it sprout all the more into our experience.

The hindrances are part of the pain of being human, so they are present in our children as much as in ourselves. Before we deal in this chapter with our children's behavioural problems, we consider the role of each hindrance in our own minds.

Let's look now at each hindrance in turn, with the exception of the third—sloth and torpor—which we investigated in Chapter 3 on boredom. In that chapter we discussed how dealing with boredom is a matter of reactivating our curiosity and sense of engagement with our surroundings, a matter of opening to the awe and wonder of any object we perceive. We also addressed boredom in children back in Chapter 3: let them be bored for a while and marvel at how it so often leads to creativity and resourcefulness.

SENSE DESIRE IN OURSELVES

'Being freed from sense desire is like being freed from debt.'
We go through phases of telling ourselves that an object, or a person, can take away our pain and make us happy, yet our craving blinds us to the full picture: the impermanence, the unsatisfactoriness and the dependent nature of any object of desire. By dependent nature, the Buddha meant that nothing exists in and of itself, for every object is completely dependent on its causes and conditions, one of these being how the object appears to our mind—which has little to do with the reality of the object. In the case of consumer goods, for example, we fail to see any object as a mere stage in a process, a process which will eventually include the end of the object's life. So, too, do we fail to predict the fading, if not the complete about-turn, in our perception of the object's attractions. For our minds, with the help of advertisers, are more likely to see each consumer good as a means to enhance our attractiveness, to achieve comfort or keep us stimulated. Such products help us to stay cool, fashionable and up with the times, or at least this is how each object appears to our minds. The Buddha

would argue that this is the very delusion that leads to *dukkha*, that is, dis-ease or suffering.

The gourmet food turns to love handles, the retail goods turn to clutter and any source of satisfying sex could never deliver consistently over the long term. Yet in the heat of our desire we seldom see any of this. Working with the hindrance of sense desire is therefore a matter of challenging ourselves to see the glorified object clearly, that is, to see its impermanence, its unsatisfactoriness and its dependent nature. Nothing out there can take away our pain for good. Nothing out there will give us lasting happiness. We can only cultivate it within us.

The antidote for inappropriate sexual desire, to consider one example of craving for sensory pleasure, as prescribed by the Buddha is a matter of seeing the person of our desire not in terms of all his superficial attractions but rather in terms of his: 'intestines, bowels, stomach, excrement, bile, phlegm, pus, blood, sweat, fat, tears, lymph, saliva, mucus, fluid of the joints, urine and the brain in the skull.' Sorry if you were eating. The Buddha was never prudish with his language but his point was, 'the body does not appear as it really is'.

SENSE DESIRE IN OUR CHILDREN

Our children are loath to admit: the ice-cream they thought would solve all their problems lasts five minutes; the toy so pined after loses its lustre within days of its purchase. Mothers everywhere know the challenge of finding a present that provides pleasure for more than a few days. Children, with the intensity of their longings, truly demonstrate the fleeting nature of our desires for sense pleasures, and the way, once satisfied, new ones come along in an endless, expensive and exhausting stream.

My children make many requests each day, particularly in the food department, and I make a point of denying them several of these requests every day. They need to learn to go without, and that they can't have everything they want. Excuse me if 'saying no occasionally' sounds too basic to even bother articulating, yet resisting pester-power is usually difficult. How often do we feel strong enough to endure the whining that 'no' brings? Almost every day we have a chance to practise a special spiritual virtue for mothers: tolerance of whining.

It's not only food. When Zac starts nagging me to buy him what he sees as the ultimate toy, which he simply *must* have, and that 'everybody else' has, I remind him of all the toys he has desperately wanted in the past and how, after only days, they languish forgotten in the toy corner. I challenge him to examine his desire so that he is less under its control.

I ask him the same questions my Buddhist teachers urge me to ask myself when I am caught in intense wanting:

- What is it that you really want from this object? What do you believe it can do for you?
- How does it feel to want this object so much?
- For how long do you think this object will make you happy?

Followed by a question of my own:

- Who will have to tidy up after you've played with this toy?

One important aspect to teach our children about craving is about the way it blinds us to other options. Caught in strong craving, we insist that only one object can make us happy. Camilla taught her animal-loving son this lesson:

Jordan, at the age of nine, got it into his head that he wanted a ferret. He researched on the internet and became more and more excited. He started setting up his bedroom and making a budget and writing lists. Meanwhile, my own research revealed ferrets need a lot of attention. It was unlikely to get on well with the cat and would probably escape into the bush behind our house—we did not have a suitable home. Yet Jordan's excitement only mounted with each new day of research.

I tried to plant some seeds of doubt in his mind, but after three weeks he had saved the money and had come to ask for our permission to buy one from the pet store. I didn't want to give him a flat no, but wanted for him to be able to see that this was not a wise decision. I explained the problems I could foresee and finally he reached an understanding that it was not realistic. I left him to have a little cry, and when I returned to him he was still really sad. He said, 'I know what you're going to say, Mum: that I should just let go of my desire for the ferret.'

But I answered: 'No, I wasn't going to say that. I just wanted to say that over three weeks you've built up in your mind the desire for this ferret. Now you're stuck in this loop: *I want the ferret, I can't have it, I want the ferret, I can't have it.* That means now you can't see any other option. Could you broaden your view at all and consider other animals? You were always interested in breeding lizards; maybe we should just investigate what lizard to buy next?'

So we ended up with another lizard. Importantly, he saw that if he stayed trapped in that loop of wanting the ferret, there would never be any relief, let alone joy. It was a lesson in how narrow our mind can become when our desires intensify and the way we stop seeing all the other potential sources of happiness. Still, I was inspired by the way he could grieve but then let go. Adults are much more likely to sulk for a long time about not getting what they want. We won't be happy until we have what we desire and won't consider other possibilities quite so readily. I wonder if it's because adults invest much more of their self-image into what they desire? They say to themselves, this object that I want is me, a representation of who I am and what I'm about.

Indeed, Buddhist teachings confirm that at the root of all craving is the desire for a strong sense of self, even though the construction of this 'self' is based on false or illusory building blocks.

ILL-WILL IN OURSELVES

'Being released from the grip of ill will is like recovering from an illness.'

If we tell ourselves that feeling angry is not okay, if we try to suppress the feeling or push it away, we only empower it. Curiously, resisting anger seems to fuel it. How much gentler we are on ourselves when we can accept the feeling of anger, not because 'we have every right to be angry', but because it is just another phenomenon arising in the mind and is by no means unique to us. After all, when we take our anger personally, seeing it as 'my' anger, we suffer all the more. Caught in 'my' anger, the false sense of self, the ego, is at its very strongest. Accepting the presence of anger does not mean we act on it by ranting and slamming doors. We do not need to fear anger but need rather to have faith in our ability to be with it, to tolerate it non-judgementally. In fact, we often find that the very act of allowing the anger to exist will, to a degree, soften it.

Of course, to be able to accept the existence of anger within us in any moment, we need to be aware that it has arisen. That is why Buddhists make a practice of noting and labelling the presence of various mind states, such as 'anger' or 'sadness'. In *Momma Zen*, a book about the struggles of motherhood from a Buddhist perspective, mother and Zen priest Karen Maezen Miller describes how she notes anger aloud:

> I lose it all the time. We all lose it all the time. The point is not that we lose our cool, the point is how quickly we find it again . . . I practise pausing, breathing and saying, 'I'm angry right now.' Or 'I'm frustrated right now.' Or 'I'm sad right now . . .' When I speak a feeling, it changes me, it changes my body, it loosens the noose and lowers the temperature . . . Spoken, these words by themselves are safe, but unspoken, they smolder into fire and brimstone.

Any claim that we should never yell or expose our anger and frustration to our children could only come from someone with no first-hand experience of parenting. Or at least no experience at my house. That is why I appreciate Karen's words that the point is not that we 'lose our cool' but 'how quickly we find it again'. Examining my own daily parenting I cannot claim my Buddhist practice has stopped me from losing my cool, but I do feel it has helped me find it again quite quickly, preventing me from wallowing in anger and self-pity for extended periods. I would even argue that for children the occasional outburst from their mother might be helpful to teach them that their actions affect others. It is my hope that my moments of unravelling might even teach them to feel empathy and healthy remorse.

With some of the challenging behaviours we confront, how realistic is it to expect ourselves never to bite back? After all, we are often tired, overburdened, or coming down with a cold—and not many children are sensitive enough to adjust their behaviour to suit their mother's current condition. I have been down the road of feeling guilty about angry outbursts, but guilt never solved the problem. Then again, we cannot afford to make yelling our standard parenting technique, just as it is not in our interests to spend hours each day feeling angry. Constant yelling takes a toll on us but also, as in the case of the boy who cried wolf, our children adjust to such regimes—they de-sensitise and start ignoring us. I speak from experience. We need to be more crafty.

Camilla recently promised her children a cycling trip round a zoo in the country three hours west of Sydney. When their day at the zoo arrived temperatures were blisteringly hot, and Camilla could imagine her children nagging for drinks and ice-creams and complaining endlessly about the heat and fatigue. Camilla gave each child an allowance and told them that each time anyone so much as mentioned the heat they would lose a dollar from their drinks-and-iceblocks money. We can always challenge ourselves to find inventive ways to avoid an embarrassing family meltdown—or over-reliance on yelling.

Of course, reactive emotions such as anger can be our most helpful teachers. An Indian man called Vijay who attends my Buddhist group from time to time has experienced an awakening. Over a year since his life-jolting experience, he claims his experience of life has changed irrevocably. Now calm, content and freed from his ego, he claims he no longer feels attachment to anything for he finally understands that, 'the self that had been doing so much seeking was a joke,' as in, there was never really a solid self running the show. He once gave a public talk about his experiences to my group, and although I have always prided myself on my scepticism, my intuition guides me to believe and trust him. In fact, several of the more sceptical in my group believe him: here is a man who has crossed over to the other side. What astounds me most about Vijay is that he attributes his experience of awakening to his determination to observe and understand his experiences with negative emotions. Anger was one of his main teachers, a teacher that took him exceptionally far. (More of my discussions with the intriguing Vijay appear in the next chapter.)

ILL-WILL IN OUR CHILDREN

Excuse the generalisation, but when plans go awry I find men prone to blaming others while women are far more likely to blame themselves—hence our battles with guilt. As a mother of sons I aspire to teach my boys to acknowledge their own role when things go wrong—hopefully also conveying the importance of patience, compassion and forgiveness for their part in any misadventures.

The other day Zac said something that really pleased me. After a spell of being short-tempered and cranky with his brother and mother, he announced, 'I'm just cranky because I'm feeling really tired.' I immediately congratulated him: despite feeling out of sorts he could still take responsibility for the events of the afternoon and, rather than become stuck in blaming others, was able to isolate a major cause. As we all know, many adults are not capable of seeing that their anger comes from fatigue, hunger or lack of down time. Pleased to have been congratulated, Zac has continued over time to explain his behaviour when such unpleasant moods strike him and this gives him a sense of perspective on his complaints.

I try to make a point of warning the boys when my fuse feels short, and explaining to them how I am feeling so they do not take my mood too personally. Any angry outburst will then be construed for what it is: the voice of a tired woman who has endured a demanding day, a woman therefore short of patience for irritating behaviour. I hope that this teaches them that our reactions are more a function of how our bodies feel, or the state of our inner world, than any external event.

An angry child focuses on blaming the world outside themself and is not likely to examine within to see how they are feeling in themself. Busy ranting about external irritants, they can be brought up short if their mother asks them, 'Just pause for a moment and see exactly how your body is feeling in this moment.' The 'pause' is a valuable technique for school-aged children and need only take a few seconds. In those moments, our attention comes back to the body, back to the present, back into spaciousness, to a place where we find perspective on whatever is happening. Our own mothers may have told us to 'count to ten' in times of anger, and in the same way, the 'pause' provides the breathing space which stops us becoming too 'carried away' with our psychological dramas.

Just as their mothers do, our children want to feel heard, understood and as though somebody cares about how they feel. So the more we can talk about the underlying feelings of a situation, the closer our bond can grow. This means that rather than jumping straight into problem-solving mode with an angry child, we might, if time allows, explore the emotions they are experiencing. So we listen to their grievance and reflect the emotions we hear: 'You sound really frustrated,' or, 'When did you start feeling so upset?' or, 'I guess you found that quite irritating.'

Make use of the full extent of our language to capture all the nuances of anger—the more specific our children can be about their feelings, the more likely they can make themselves understood and gain a sense of control over what they feel. We can equip our children to specify whether they feel: inconvenienced, put out, bothered, cranky, irritated, disturbed, irate, mad, misunderstood, frustrated, upset, exasperated, furious, fuming or neglected. For the sake of balance, we might teach them adjectives to describe positive feelings as well.

After the anger has died down, it can be worth asking your child some questions about their episode. What beliefs do they hold about the situation? Could these beliefs be disputed? Did the anger help the situation? Is there a more effective approach or attitude?

ANXIETY AND WORRY IN OURSELVES

'Freedom from anxiety and worry is like freedom from slavery.'
The Buddha equates the experiences of anxiety and worry to slavery. When our minds are restless and disturbed, our thoughts push us around, control our every impulse and generally leave us at their mercy. We believe everything our thoughts say, and they present us with few choices: it is pure slavery. The heart of the problem is our rejection of the present moment, our inability, or refusal, to find inside us any acceptance of the way things are now.

Always needing more, always seeking improvements, always trying to 'get somewhere', our mind becomes a place of tumult. Meanwhile, the tension in our body mounts until we become a mass of knots, which only exacerbates our original problem. Despite what we believe when in the grip of this hindrance, most of our suffering at such times is self-created.

In Chapter 7, which addressed fear, worry and anxiety, we looked at antidotes such as accepting a degree of unsatisfactoriness, reducing our attachment to our preferences and letting go of some of our attachment to control. When we are capable of any of these actions, we are more available to the present moment and we have several choices about how to inhabit our present more fully. We might return to awareness of our breath, of the tension in our body, of the sounds around us, of our visual surroundings. We might open to the simple, easily overlooked joys around us, be they in nature or in the abundance of what we have. We might consciously relax all our muscles. Or we may choose to observe the tumult of our minds with non-judgemental awareness. If we feel clear-headed, we might be capable of switching our mindset to one of gratitude or humour. The tranquillity that accompanies the concentrated mind is the antidote for our habitual 'monkey mind', so focusing our mind in the present is the most reliable way to rediscover peace of mind.

Anxious worriers can benefit greatly from meditation. My friend Lisa, a mother who suffers from intermittent anxious depression, sees a psychologist who suggests she meditates twice a day, whether she is suffering or well. For her meditation Lisa listens to a CD that guides the meditator through a 'body scan' similar to the one I do with Zac, described in Chapter 6. With the help of medication, Lisa has recently recovered from several harrowing weeks of depressed mood. Her recovery came halfway through a 'second honeymoon' alone with her husband on a tropical island. Back to her normal, enthusiastic self, she tells me on the phone that the holiday gave her additional time to spend meditating, and she feels sure that the deep mental and physical relaxation she experienced was a large contributor to her recovery.

The hindrance of 'anxiety and worry' includes our nagging feelings of guilt. Buddhist teachings are in favour of remorse when we have made a mistake or harmed others. Remorse is about being honest and clear about the effects of our actions, about taking responsibility. When we exaggerate our remorse in an obsessive fashion, becoming stuck, the remorse becomes guilt, an unhelpful mind state we use to punish and shame ourselves, such that our minds know no rest. Buddhist practice requires of us a preparedness to forgive ourselves again and again and again.

ANXIETY AND WORRY IN OUR CHILDREN

One characteristic that has always surprised me in children, even pre-schoolers, is how important it is to never appear foolish in front of others. Since being laughed at is so humiliating, the prospect is definitely something to worry about. It is easy for adults to forget the pressure on children to be all-rounders, or at least to never make a fool of oneself in any area, and this gives many children a lot to worry about. As adults, we have all been allowed to specialise and focus on where our abilities have taken us in life, whereas children must follow every aspect of a wide curriculum. Participating in sport may be nerve-wrackingly embarrassing for a certain type of child but it is compulsory—as is public speaking, socialising in the playground and performing academically in a wide range of subjects.

Overall, the breadth of a school curriculum is positive for most children, giving everyone a chance to work on their weaknesses and explore all kinds of strengths. While few of us would exert undue pressure on our children to excel in every single area, it can be tricky choosing just the right amount of pressure to apply, if any: the less motivated child needs a different kind of parent to the self-starter. Sadly, many modern parents forget the importance for young schoolchildren of interest and enjoyment. With too much pressure to perform, from too young an age, we program our children for a life of worry and anxiety—if they don't give up altogether.

One often-overlooked risk is that our children start to identify too closely with their performance at school. Yet they are not their results. If their whole identity hangs on their performance at school—or on the sporting field—then their self-acceptance throughout their lives will always be conditional and they will have a lot more to be anxious about. If we can take every opportunity to convey to our child that our love is unconditional—such that our child never feels they need to earn love or prove themself—then the parent allows their child a strong foundation of self-acceptance. Such love with no strings attached is the very meaning of Buddhist non-attachment in the context of parenting.

As I mentioned above in the case of adults, guilt is an aspect of this hindrance and children, like us, suffer from feelings of guilt and shame when they have done wrong. My Zac, a text-book firstborn in some ways, is always quick to apologise and make amends. He can sink into instant despondency when he realises a wrongdoing, so I am at pains to remind him of what a good person he is overall. His Buddha Nature is never far from the surface so it is easy to provide evidence for his innate kindness and integrity.

I need to talk to Zac at such times in a way that prevents him from becoming stuck in his guilt. This means that as soon as any bad behaviour has been addressed, I switch to pointing out his good qualities. I also point out that any unskilful behaviour is not who he is, and is by no means unique to him. It was just something that 'came up', that comes up for everybody, and the important lesson for him is to understand the harm and deal with his emotions more skilfully in the future. As a child, and unlike many adults, Zac is impressively capable of then dropping the whole incident and opening to the next moment in his life, unburdened by the past.

DOUBT IN OURSELVES

'Passing beyond doubt is like completing a perilous desert crossing.'
'Doubt is a hindrance?' you may ask. Didn't the Buddha warn us never to take for granted what others told us, to approach every moment with a questioning attitude and never to settle for the accepted wisdom of others unless we have tested it for ourselves? The Buddha certainly shared our Western value of critical thinking and scepticism. Zen Buddhists even have a saying: 'Great doubt, great awakening; little doubt, little awakening; no doubt, no awakening.'

So how can doubt be a hindrance? While the experience of doubt can be helpful by keeping us open and alert to all we digest, it can definitely be hindering as well. We experience unhelpful doubt, for example, when after considerable hand-wringing we still cannot reach a decision. Ongoing doubt can render us disengaged from our lives, cynical or fearful of any commitment—all a far cry from our ideal of feeling passionate and taking joy in what we do.

Like any hindrance, we empower ourselves when we can label the experience: 'doubt.' This instantly puts some distance between ourselves and the experience, allowing us to observe it rather than go on its journey quite so much. Observing doubt is an education as we watch the old stories (*This is just like that terrible time I . . .*), beliefs (*I'm no good at this kind of thing . . .*) and body sensations (frowning, shoulder-tensing) that accompany it. Ironically, the antidote to doubt can be doubt itself. We can always doubt our doubts, asking: Do these doubting thoughts represent The Great and Unchanging Truth? Do we need to necessarily believe them? Are they even that important? Do they help me get the job done or are they just a habit-fuelled phenomenon of the mind? Focused concentration on the task at hand is another way to silence unhelpful doubt.

Self-doubt is a phenomenon that haunts most women. How many times, particularly in those early years, did we collapse in exhaustion, concluding that motherhood was completely beyond our capacities? In our paid work too, we may have panicked in the face of a challenge, feeling anxiety over whether we could meet its demands. Every day I sit down to write this book I am plagued with doubts about whether I will have anything to write today. Every day I come up with something, but that does not stop me from feeling doubtful the very next day. I have learned to scoff at these thoughts, ignore them and press on.

If we are in the habit of perpetual self-evaluation, always worrying about whether we are good enough, then self-doubt will be a frequent visitor. We tend to panic as soon as self-doubt arises rather than seeing it as a passing mind state like any other. Self-doubt feels like a dangerous threat to the ego so can cause extreme emotional reactions. Yet read the biography of any successful person and we realise that everyone experiences self-doubt, for insecurities abound in all of us, even if some have to dig deeper to reveal them.

Self-doubt is an inevitable part of spiritual practice. Seeing ourselves behave unskilfully time after time, we can occasionally give up on our potential to make any progress. The antidote to doubt about the Buddha's teachings and our personal capacity to practise them is faith. While many flinch at the very mention of the word 'faith', assuming it means blind obedience, in Buddhism faith is not about following dogma and gurus, but rather relates to our own capacity to practise the teachings. It is faith in ourselves and in how much the teachings can help us. It helps to ask ourselves what nourishes such faith. Many Buddhists would answer that spending time with advanced practitioners and teachers best nurtures their faith, as can the study of the Buddha's teachings. For some, building faith is a matter of increasing their commitment to meditation and watching the results, such as increased calm and presence, throughout their day.

DOUBT IN OUR CHILDREN

One way our children can strengthen their backbone and avoid being tossed about by all the competing views around them is if we teach them to trust and rely on their own inner voice. Teaching them the skill of turning inward to listen to their own intuition, their own conscience, rather than always deferring to their elders, superiors or peers, helps to establish in them a strong inner compass. So when our children have a decision to make, we resist the temptation to jump in and make it for them and, rather, help them to explore their own views on the situation. We provide opportunities for our children to practise checking in with their own mind. Of course, there are times when they are younger when we need to step in and steer, but if mothers show some faith in a child's ability to make their own choices in a few areas, the child learns to trust their own mind more.

Similarly, when our children have a personal problem to solve, we help them to explore the problem and find their own answers rather than telling them what to do. While we can remind them of our core values, such as kindness to others and the need to avoid harm, our child gains experience in the important life-skill of solving problems. It helps to ask open-ended questions—that is, questions with answers that do not lead only to 'yes' or 'no' but to fuller, more thoughtful answers. We might point out the observable facts of a situation but leave our children to form their own opinions and make their own judgements. We might also listen more so that our children can explore their ideas uninterrupted. When we talk less, we create space for our children's thoughts to develop.

When the hindrance of doubt for our children takes the form of self-doubt, our reflex action may be to heap unearned praise upon them, complimenting them all day long and downplaying their weaknesses. Yet gratuitous praise, or praise that is not specific, will do little over the long run to convince a child of their worth. Eminent psychologist Martin Seligman is one of several commentators who point to the 'self-esteem movement', where children are praised and rewarded regardless of the quality of their achievements, for the recent explosion in the number of depressed children. If a child can attract praise with minimal effort, why try any harder? Without the need to make any effort, they lose the opportunity to feel proud of hard-earned achievements and what these could have contributed to their self-worth.

Seligman argues that in constant pandering to a child's self-esteem we focus only on how a child feels, and overlook what the child does. He believes true self-esteem comes from 'mastery, persistence, overcoming frustration and boredom, and meeting challenge'. We could see our generation's preoccupation with bolstering our children's self-esteem as part of our general effort to protect children from any negative feelings, even though negative feelings are a natural and often constructive part of life. As Martin Seligman writes in *The Optimistic Child*:

> In order for your child to experience mastery, it is necessary for him to fail, to feel bad, and to try again repeatedly until success occurs. None of these steps can be circumvented. Failure and feeling bad are necessary building blocks for ultimate success and feeling good.

I see his view as complementing a Buddhist perspective, where we help our children to be clear-sighted and honest about their strengths, weaknesses and paths to improving. We can speak diplomatically yet truthfully with our children rather than tip-toeing around what we perceive as their fragile ego. We make a suitable fuss over their talents and triumphs, but when they underperform we together identify what needs more practice. Depending on who our child is, we may need to be highly sensitive with our language, or go to some length to identify their special skill in life, but our children need to be able to trust our praise.

One way to challenge self-doubt in our child is by asking them to explain the steps involved in their latest achievement. By talking us through these precise steps, they start to see for themselves that the result was not a matter of luck but rather, traceable to their own skills or decisions. 'What exactly did you do to win player of the match?' we might ask. Or, 'How did you come up with that idea for your project?'

Parents do model to their children ways to deal with success and failure. Do we explain our victories as a result of luck and our failures as the result of our incompetence? In other words, do we dismiss our achievements and beat ourselves up for our failures? The optimistic, supportive atmosphere we seek to cultivate in our homes needs to encompass ourselves too. It is part of a compassionate—and honest—relationship with ourselves to celebrate our successes and take some credit rather than seeing the value only in others and never in ourselves. Stephanie Dowrick sees a strong link between the self-esteem of a parent and their child, as she wrote in an article entitled, 'Happy children, happy parents':

> In a society like ours, the experience of 'enough' can be tough for children to grasp. Feeling 'good enough' can seem especially elusive. But this is something that really is best taught and learned through example, so in deepening your children's grasp and vision of happiness, you cannot fail to grow more reliably content yourself.

It appears that believing in our own adequacy is an excellent service to our child.

WHEN WORKING WITH ANY OF THE HINDRANCES...

Importantly, we pay attention to the times when a hindrance is absent, or in the Buddha's words: *When sense desire is present, a monk knows,*

'There is sense desire in me,' or when sense desire is not present, he knows, 'There is no sense desire in me.'

The Buddha challenges us to consider how it feels when the hindrance we grapple with is absent. Note the comparison. How does it affect the way our body feels? How does it affect the quality of our mindfulness of the present? We take note of the difference, and our memory of that feeling becomes an incentive for letting go of the hindrance in the future as we gradually realise we can be so much more than we habitually see ourselves.

The Buddha taught there are two antidotes common to every hindrance: Noble Friendship and Suitable Conversation. Noble Friendship refers to the need to associate with those who inspire us to a higher way of being. We can see them as experienced role models who have made progress in overcoming any of the hindrances. Alcoholics Anonymous springs to mind as a group who harness the power of Noble Friendship: members stand on the shoulders of those who have made progress in conquering their addiction. As mothers, this might mean cultivating at least some friendships with women who seek to rise above society's habitual tendencies to greed, anger, dullness, worry and rumination.

The second antidote common to all five hindrances is Suitable Conversation, whereby we steer clear of topics which compromise our integrity—that is, from gossiping, criticising others, denigrating ourselves, complaining and endlessly ruminating. Rather, we pursue topics that might enrich our minds, particularly topics that help us in our spiritual practice.

Inquiry

• Do you approach spiritual practice determined to change yourself? Do you strive to change your children? Do you ever stop to consider that both you and your children are already whole and that peace lies in dealing with the hindrances that obscure our fundamental Buddha Nature?

- Do you tend to suppress, block or deny the experience of unpleasant emotions? If so, would it be possible to accept their temporary presence with open curiosity instead?

Sense desire

- In the grip of desire for sensory pleasures, are you able to challenge your perception of the object and so understand its unreliable, impermanent nature?
- Do you make a point of often saying 'no' to your children? Do you ever teach them the nature of craving (endless, unrealistic) and the value of letting go of at least *some* of our endlessly arising cravings?
- Can you see the way strong craving blinds you to the numerous alternative options that may exist?
- Can you trace some of your stronger cravings back to your need to construct a self?

Ill-will

- Do you allow yourself to 'be with' anger, as opposed to acting on it or suppressing it?
- Do you teach your child to pause and check in with the state of their body when they fall into a dark mood?
- Do you dive straight into problem-solving mode every time your child is upset or can you, at times, pause and offer words that allow your child to feel heard and understood?
- Can you find a chance to debrief an angry episode from your child? To calmly analyse how helpful their response was in solving the problem?

Anxiety and worry

- In times of anxiety and worry, can you challenge yourself to take a step back to observe your thoughts and admit they are not necessarily The Truth?
- If you are prone to worry, can you spend more time in the present moment instead of dreaming up future nightmare scenarios?
- As a parent, do you emphasise the importance of learning, being interested and enjoying rather than only high marks?
- Have you taught your child the difference between remorse (a simple recognition of any harm done) and guilt (ongoing shame)?

Doubt

- What role does doubt play in your spiritual practice? Is there too much? Too little?
- Have you developed the skill of disputing unhelpful thoughts of self-doubt?
- What can you do to increase your faith in your capacity to practise the teachings?
- In addressing self-doubt in a child, is your praise honest, specific and trust-worthy?
- Have you acknowledged any link between how you treat your own successes/failures and how your child will treat their own?

•

- Are you ever mindful of how it feels when a hindrance is absent?
- Have you considered the role of Noble Friendship in your life? The need to spend time with mothers who inspire you?

- Have you considered the role of Suitable Conversation in your life? The need to be mindful of how what you talk about affects, or reflects, your way of being in the world?

CHAPTER 10

happiness

REMEMBER WHEN WE THOUGHT that having children would make us happy? I had always loved children: how much more would I love my own? Many of us, in those early days of motherhood, felt somewhat bewildered at just how 'not happy' we could feel after hours of domestic chores and child care. Interestingly, Professor Daniel Gilbert, author and professor of psychology at Harvard University, asserts that children definitely do not make us happier. He even argues that most couples experience a marked increase in happiness only after their children have grown up and left home. Quoting from an article Gilbert wrote for *Time* magazine:

> Psychologists have measured how people feel as they go about their daily activities, and have found that people are less happy when they are interacting with their children than when they are eating, exercising, shopping or watching television. Indeed, an act of parenting makes most people about as happy as an act of housework. Economists have modeled the impact of many variables on people's overall happiness and have consistently found that children have only a small impact. A small negative impact.

For many mothers such research is not particularly surprising: they readily admit that preparing children for school is not fun, and neither is nagging them to clean their rooms, do their homework and get ready for bed. All the same, most of us remain pleased with our decision to become parents. Gilbert believes this is because we focus so heavily on the brief moments of joy, such as when our children tell us they love us. We rationalise the enormous costs rather than admit we made a misjudgement about what would make us happy. The true reason we had children, he believes, is because our DNA drove us to.

I am inclined to agree with Gilbert: on a minute-by-minute basis, for me, unpleasant minutes with my children probably outnumber pleasant ones by a small increment. I enjoy my conversations with the boys and I savour moments to watch them and absorb their beauty, but I do spend most of my time with them begging them to take more responsibility for themselves, or asking them to do things they have no interest in doing. My children have always resisted, for example, the simple act of going to sleep at the end of the day, so I need to make every request at this time of day at least three times. Come to think of it, I need to make every request at least three times no matter what time of day it is.

I would also agree with Gilbert that the joyful moments are so powerful that they easily whitewash the whole experience of motherhood: on any day I could declare becoming a mother the best decision I ever made—and I mean it. Zac is so loving and well-intentioned. Alex is so hilarious and engaging. My smile is never so genuine as when prompted by these two characters. Parental pride is definitely one of the most enjoyable emotions, even though it is not always appropriate to reveal too much of this emotion to others.

So crossing children off the list of what might make us consistently happy, what is left? For most of my life I expected to find happiness from big, splashy events: a financial windfall, winning a competition, finding the perfect job, a romance, some recognition, an overseas trip. As I grew older I learned that such occasions were not the most reliable sources of happiness for me, especially not any kind of lasting happiness. I was often surprised to experience a sense of anticlimax at the arrival of such events, or sometimes nothing more than immense relief that a strong craving was finally satisfied. Such experiences sometimes stirred up my mind, triggering insomnia or anxiety about how long I could hold on to the situation.

For me, the best lesson about growing older has been my increased understanding that contentment is something I cultivate within myself and for which I need not rely on external circumstances—which are unreliable and will always change. Becoming happy is about learning to look deeply into the faces of my children, learning to enjoy my walk to the post office, and remembering to pause and absorb the beauty of any moment. When I am able to find the joy in simple tasks, I condition my mind into one that is more calm and content. Nourishing my inner life—through meditation, conscious awareness of the present moment and cultivating compassion for others—is a far safer bet on happiness than trying to control my external conditions.

Another prominent Gilbert who does not see children as the path to happiness, at least for herself, is Elizabeth Gilbert, author of *Eat Pray Love*. I accidentally put my whole life on hold to read her captivating memoir of a spiritual quest spanning Italy, India and Indonesia, a quest following her difficult decision to leave her marriage and all its prospects for starting a family. As someone I admire greatly for her worldliness and her impressive achievements in writing, it helped me in my own quest, to read her hard-won insights on the topic of happiness:

> I have searched frantically for contentment for so many years in so many ways, and all these acquisitions and accomplishments—they run you down in the end. Life, if you keep chasing it so hard, will drive you to death . . . You have to admit that you can't catch it. That you're not supposed to catch it. At some point, as Richard keeps telling me, you gotta let go and sit still and allow contentment to come to you.

If we could take her words to heart, we might save ourselves a tremendous amount of the hard work required in 'chasing life'. Still,

I have some way to go before I realise, once and for all, the truth that happiness needs to come from within me. I do still rub my hands together in eager anticipation of what delights the world might still have in store for me: a new interest, a fascinating client, a life-changing experience. Yet it is in fact all my beliefs about the worth of these events—and beliefs all come from inside me—that create the happiness rather than any particular event itself. By making time to 'let go', 'sit still' and 'allow contentment to come', I shape my mind into one which is more likely to react to the events of my life in a skilful, non-grasping way.

For the busy, modern mother, our lives are so full of activity, distraction and stimulation that it is all the more difficult to quieten our minds. The challenge for us is to react to all these demands skilfully, with a minimum of clinging and aversion. Equanimity, or non-attachment, was the Buddha's answer to the happiness puzzle. One Buddhist friend, Jen, uses a mantra of her own throughout her day: 'I don't mind what happens.' While she might have a favoured scenario in mind—a tidy house, an empty in-tray, friendly interactions—she tries not to be overly attached to any of these. She can handle deviations from the grand plan—or at least, that is her vision.

RISING ABOVE PETTY IRRITATIONS

How do you feel as you rush through your errands? As you tear through the supermarket, visit the bank, post your mail, do you remember to be present? Are you able to be calm? Asking myself these questions as I rush through the streets, I have looked within and, on occasion, found impatience, gritted teeth and tension. This is doubtless because I have rated my errands as unpleasant activities which need to be out of my way. Yet how will I ever find any kind of lasting contentment if I keep dividing the activities of my life into 'enjoyable' and 'boring'?

The challenge we face is to find some enjoyment in all our activities. On my walk to the post office I can enjoy the exercise, the fact that I am able to walk freely and without pain. I can study the faces I pass, feel the subtle breeze, appreciate the opportunity to practise mindfulness, and the not-small miracle that I live in a place where the infrastructure exists that allows me to send a letter. I could notice the details of my surroundings, or observe my stream of thoughts with conscious awareness. It is perfectly possible for my scurry to the post office to be a joyful interlude.

It is always harder when we are worried about squeezing our errands in before the school pick-up, when we find long queues, or when our plans for the day are disrupted—and we always seem to work with at least one of these challenges. Yet surely our spiritual life is more important than these small grievances. When our spiritual practice is strong we can rise above these irritations: we are unassailable. Nothing can pull us down, for we have a spacious perspective, a bigger picture in mind.

Although anyone can see the value in rising above the frustrations of daily life, few people do. As Camilla noted: 'It always hits me while walking around the shopping centre how miserable people look. There's not a lot of smiling going on—especially round Christmas time.'

Camilla, like many Buddhists, will often send strangers feelings of lovingkindness as she walks around the streets, and who could deny this is better for your karma than clenching your teeth and cursing under your breath, 'Get out of my way, old lady'? Sending others lovingkindness as we walk around our suburb is an excellent way to make our minds more spacious and compassionate. Camilla adds:

I smile at people: the cashiers, sales staff, people on the street. If I offer a genuine smile to someone, I might just be catching them at a point where contact with another human being shifts their mood—and I've been on the receiving end of such smiles. Who knows, their next interaction might be more giving as well.

Errands can become spiritual practice. As I hand my parcel to the postal clerk I wonder if all day she has felt 'unseen', a cog in a wheel, a means to others' ends. How appreciated does she feel for her long day on her feet? If I can say something friendly to her or, however briefly, engage with her in a way that makes her feel acknowledged, then we both feel lifted.

Camilla shows us how we can turn queue-frustration into something more wholesome:

Recently I was in a queue and the cashier was really slow. My anger started rising but then I caught myself. I began to cultivate feelings of understanding for her approach to her work, imagining possible causes—and it did not take much imagination. By the time I reached the front of the queue I was able to smile and sympathetically remark on how busy it was. I'm sure I left the supermarket feeling better than if I had let the anger run its course.

SYMPATHETIC JOY

One tested Buddhist technique for increasing our capacity for happiness is to practise sympathetic joy. My sister Amanda has a capacity for sympathetic joy, an ability to take pleasure in the good fortune of others, that often leaves me gobsmacked. I feel touched, inspired and personally challenged by her ability to take genuine delight from seeing others flourish. I also feel deep gratitude for the sympathetic joy she shows for me: she is my sister after all, so jealousy, competition or envy would hardly be bizarre. Yet Amanda loves to report any positive feedback she hears about either of her sisters; she takes a keen interest in how our lives are going; and she goes to great lengths to watch my choir perform, even if I have not invited her. When this kind of behaviour comes from a sister it is easy to tell whether it is genuine, and in her case it definitely is.

Growing up with my younger sister Amanda, she excelled in the very subjects at school that I struggled with, she was far better looking and far more popular. Even my dog liked her better than me. A competitive youngster with big-sister pride to protect, I was jealous as all hell. I am sure I failed her completely at providing sympathetic joy for any of her victories, and this is why I feel so profoundly grateful, and humbled, that she has been able to provide it so whole-heartedly for me. If she had any tendencies to pettiness she would have every reason to withhold sympathetic joy from me, yet her reluctance to do so has worked wonders for her karma: she is so clearly full of joy over events that have nothing to do with her own ego structure. Many humans are not capable of that.

Sympathetic joy is one of the four components of love that the Buddha encouraged us to cultivate. The other three are compassion, lovingkindness and equanimity. If we are to truly love another person, then we need to ensure all four components are present. For example, there needs to be a balance between sympathetic joy and compassion. If we are only capable of sympathetic joy in a relationship then we are a fair-weather friend who will disappear when challenges arise. Yet many among us have experienced the opposite: more insecure friends love you when you are down but cannot cope when you start to emerge from your slump—they can do compassion but sympathetic joy is the challenge for them.

Equanimity is about providing a sense of balance to our experience of love. If a loved one excels, for example, we feel delighted but we do not feel attachment to their achievement: it feels like a bonus, a treat, rather than something we insist upon. With equanimity, our sympathetic joy is not at risk of adopting a dizzy or hysterical tone. Tibetan Buddhists in particular expand this definition of equanimity to capture the idea that our love needs to be for all living beings rather than only family members and close friends. They argue that our love can only be genuine and free of attachment if we are capable of extending it to those who are not in our inner circle of loved ones.

An interesting variation on the usual lovingkindness meditation practised by Buddhists, where we wish people well, is to make the focus sympathetic joy. This is a matter of cultivating feelings of joy for the good fortune of others, starting with yourself, followed by someone you love, a neutral person, a difficult person, then all living beings. We imagine others feeling joyful, for whatever reason, and share in their happiness. This is a reliable way to suffuse our mind with joy as we meditate. Similarly, we could base our meditation on cultivating compassion towards others where we focus on what might be difficult for each individual. As for equanimity, all meditation is about cultivating equanimity, that is, feelings of peacefulness, calm and non-attachment.

It is interesting that the different schools of Buddhism often have a different level of emphasis on love. The Tibetans give it enormous emphasis, with the Dalai Lama saying, 'My religion is kindness.' In my own tradition of Insight, which is the non-monastic or Western form of Theravada Buddhism, many teachers place far less emphasis on love in favour of cultivating wisdom. There are definite exceptions to this, such as the great teacher Sharon Salzberg in the United States, whose energy is, for the most part, dedicated to teaching the cultivation of lovingkindness, compassion, sympathetic joy and equanimity.

I have heard some of my favourite Insight teachers argue that to practise lovingkindness meditation would be to impose an emotion on yourself that was not naturally there and that it is best to practise it only when it arises spontaneously. For a while I agreed with this yet noticed in myself a disturbing lack of positive feelings towards some parents in the playground. There was definitely something missing in my practice—yet through lovingkindness meditation, this aspect of practice was easy enough to reignite. After all, the Buddha said in his Sermon at Rajagaha:

> Gifts are great . . . meditations and religious exercises pacify the heart, comprehension of the truth leads to Nirvana, but greater than all is lovingkindness. As the light of the moon is sixteen times stronger than the light of all the stars, so lovingkindness is sixteen times more efficacious in liberating the heart than all other religious accomplishments taken together.

I am happy to report that these days I am perfectly capable of experiencing sympathetic joy *and* lovingkindness *and* compassion *and* equanimity for my sister Amanda.

BALANCE IN OUR LIFESTYLES

Our chances of feeling happy in our daily life are greatly threatened if we do not have a few basics in place. A close friend was relating to me a conversation she had with her perpetually stressed husband, in which he gravely announced that he might have depression. My friend was incredulous. 'Oh no you don't, buddy!' she replied with a viciousness that surprised even herself. 'You work a twelve-hour day in a stressful job, smoke, drink, get no exercise, eat poorly and barely sleep. Of course you feel rotten!'

Her husband did not have depression but, as my friend diagnosed, his lack of attention to the basics of well-being in his life—diet, rest, exercise—precluded any chance for the spontaneous arising of calm or contentment.

How we eat makes a huge contribution to how happy we can be. Not only do certain types of food, in the right amounts, make us happier, but our whole relationship to food can be quite a preoccupation. As discussed in Chapter 1, based on his own experience of the extremes, the Buddha taught a Middle Way between overindulgence in sensory pleasures and severe self-discipline. His teachings help us to steer ourselves back onto a middle path when we have drifted towards an extreme.

The area of diet is a good example of where we ignore many important causes and conditions that might help us break out of destructive habits. When on a diet, or even just watching our weight, we obsess over what food passes our lips: all our attention is on the food, or on resisting temptation. Yet many find it more useful to look more deeply into what drives them to food, such as the way we use food to comfort a wide range of unpleasant mind states including fear, anxiety, loneliness, boredom and sadness.

If we have ever practised paying attention to what is going on within us from moment to moment, we know that all these mind states do eventually pass. Yet our initial aversion, or even panic, when we first see such mind states arise drives us to the refuge of food, even though the cure is so temporary. The quick-fix provided by food stops us considering other more constructive options for comforting ourselves: be they yoga stretches, a minute of meditation, calling a friend, writing in a diary or focusing on the job at hand.

Camilla has faced the challenge of letting go of a substance far more addictive than chocolate bars:

The process of giving up smoking always made me so cranky that my husband banned me from ever giving up again. I've read that some heroin addicts manage to give up heroin, but can't seem to give up smoking. I started smoking at fourteen when I was probably going off the rails. Smoking was a friend and so I formed an emotional attachment. It was a constant, so if at 2 am my dad arrived home drunk and loud I could always sneak out my window and have a cigarette on the roof. It was also a way to belong with the rebels at school. I had conformed in so many ways so smoking was a chance to rebel. I managed to quit through my pregnancies because I always knew I could start up again. I could deal with a temporary giving-up but forever was another matter.

The whole time I was giving up I told myself I 'should' not smoke—so I was trying to give up using only will power and the power of 'should not'. Yet my mind was completely consumed with wanting this thing that I should not have. I tended to last three weeks and then be so angry with everyone around me that I had to light up again.

I began investigating the Four Noble Truths, and how craving causes suffering but that cessation, or the end of suffering, was possible. I watched the process: craving would build for the cigarette, then I would go outside (I never smoked in the house), light up, start smoking and experience complete cessation of craving. In fact, in that moment I experienced cessation of all my cravings. Then, within half an hour, I wanted another cigarette. The overriding craving was for nicotine and that craving would disappear, but I woke up to the illusion that with the disappearance of the nicotine craving, all my other worries and responsibilities disappeared as well.

How many of us experience the same feelings of a temporary 'cessation of all our cravings' when we take refuge in chocolate, cake or chips? Chomping on a chocolate bar, we lose ourselves in a dreamy present moment, free from our usual state of craving. Camilla continues:

> I became curious about what exactly I was craving and saw that it wasn't the cigarette, which was not all that pleasant in itself, but that sense of cessation of craving, the feeling of relief. Whenever I felt overwhelmed or out of control, which is often for a working mother of three, I'd have a cigarette.
>
> I noticed my other cravings: to have a 'self', to feel okay about myself, about my parenting abilities, about the state of the house, about my marriage and my finances.
>
> Through being more present to the experience of smoking, I discovered that many aspects of smoking were unpleasant: the smell, the isolation from my family as I stood outside, the mess of the ash. I started seeing it more clearly for what it was. I began asking, can I find this feeling of relief from another source? I could see this relentless process of craving-relief-craving-relief that could go on endlessly.
>
> The next time I tried to give up smoking I decided to use mindfulness of breathing and just be with the craving, and focused my attention on how unpleasant the craving was. So rather than suppress the craving, panic or distract myself, I would just note 'craving'. So I practised being very present with the craving, with no 'shoulds'.

I would also use the teaching of impermanence to tell myself, *this craving will be very strong but it will pass*—and it did. I didn't get angry, because I stopped feeling like I was deprived.

Part of me never believed that I could give up but now it has been five years. It was a matter of being really honest with myself about what was going on.

We can apply Camilla's discoveries to any of the addictions we battle: be they overindulging in food, shopping, drinking or even working. Camilla turned inward to examine the causes and conditions behind her smoking and eventually triumphed. She asked the important question: What do I really want right now?

Mindfulness around food can help us to slow down and savour each mouthful rather than compulsively rushing the food down. How often we forget to enjoy it and feel grateful to the innumerable people involved in making it available to us.

I can boast that I have successfully given up my daily mid-afternoon chocolate bar, but should confess that this was probably the result of a frightening ultimatum from my dentist rather than any spiritual awakening.

AWAKENING

As we know, the Buddha awakened, or became enlightened. The important though oft-neglected question is, 'Awakened to what?' or, 'Enlightened about what?'

The Buddha awakened to what he called dependent arising, the fact that all phenomena in our world are dependent on other phenomena. Nothing can exist on its own because every single thing, without exception, relies for its existence on something else. Everything exists,

including our thoughts, feelings and behaviours, as a result of causes
and conditions. In the famous words of the Buddha:

> When this is, that is
> This arising, that arises
> When this is not, that is not
> This ceasing, that ceases.

In other words, the Buddha discovered the *conditionality* of all
phenomena. This may seem obvious: at a rational level we can see
life operating as a long stream of cause and effect. Look at history.
Look at science. There are reasons behind everything that happens.
The teaching of dependent arising might even seem a little under-
whelming, yet this discovery was what the Buddha awakened to.
Buddhist scriptures are full of spiritual seekers achieving immediate
enlightenment on hearing the Buddha impart this teaching. It is the
key to liberation from recurring patterns of stress and anguish, yet
we struggle to understand it on a deep enough level.

Our perceptions of others, of ourselves and of objects tend to be
frozen, fixed, and failing to take into account the interconnected nature
of all things. Nothing exists in and of itself for all is conditioned,
dependent or contingent on causes and conditions. Since everything
is in process, there is nothing worth clinging to, for everything will
change. Yet we live our lives in a way that does not recognise this
basic truth.

Seeing processes rather than fixed objects requires more complex
understanding than we are prepared to exercise. It feels easier to view
the world in simplistic or dualistic terms: then we can just live on
automatic pilot, even though we lose the opportunity to see clearly
along with the potential to save ourselves considerable pain.

To take an everyday example of a failure to understand dependent arising, we might judge ourselves negatively for shrieking hysterically at the children and decide, in that moment, that we are a bad mother—or that we have bad children. We tend to see only the shrieking and not the causes and conditions, even though non-judgementally considering the causes and conditions would be far more constructive. Some of the many *causes* might relate to: nature, nurture, culture, history, gender, fear or habit. Some of the *conditions* surrounding our yelling might be: a feeling of irritability, the sluggishness of our body, the surrounding chaos, the fact that we're running late, or feeling unappreciated. If we work with the causes and conditions for our outburst we are likely to have more success in adopting a cool-headed, compassionate approach for the future than if we only see the yelling by itself.

The Buddha listed four causes that we tend to mistakenly assume to be behind what happens to us. The first is that we assume an event occurs solely because of me: I cause everything. The second misconception is that everything happens because of others (which for some includes God): that is, we blame others when something goes wrong or we give them all the credit when something goes well. In the third case, we oscillate between options one and two: some moments blaming ourselves, the next blaming others, in a back-and-forth pattern. Fourth, we might see everything as accidental, random, without cause, or as pure luck. Whichever cause we select, we tend to come up with very definite ideas about highly complex situations.

Do not feel discouraged if you feel confused, ambivalent or as though you might be missing something in your understanding of dependent arising. We can all expect to feel confusion, doubt or vagueness for the Buddha taught that if we truly understood this teaching we would be enlightened.

Investigating dependent arising in our lives

In search of a more balanced lifestyle, Camilla decided to make a radical change to her life based on the teaching of dependent arising:

> I have been concentrating on the teaching of dependent arising for quite some time and trying to make it real in my life, so I have become very aware of the importance of conditions in our lives. I no longer see myself as someone who acts autonomously, for my practice shows me how all my behaviour is conditioned by other things.
>
> I was not happy with the way I was feeling and behaving as a mother, but rather than condemn myself and feel guilty I focused on my conditions, and this led to a major decision. We decided to leave Sydney and move to the country. A tree change.
>
> I felt that moving to a small town where housing and schooling were more affordable would free me from such a time-consuming commitment to the paid workforce and set up the conditions for me to be a more attentive mother, wife, friend and member of the community. It would also give me more time for meditation, study and spiritual friendships.
>
> To live in this area of Sydney with three children takes an enormous amount of money, and for my husband to be working six days a week, and me four, has been too much. I just couldn't find any balance. I was becoming more and more tired, stressed and disappointed in myself. Working four days, I had to give up the things that meant the most to me, such as the voluntary work I did for the children's school and for my Buddhist group. I became stressed when the children came anywhere near me with

simple requests for attention. Even housework, which I generally see as an enjoyable opportunity to practise mindfulness, became stressful. One condition in particular was increasingly absent: the physical energy that might have allowed me to enjoy the daily two hours of housework.

I found I could keep it all running provided everyone was well but the minute anyone fell sick—and my children never got sick at the same time—then the whole system collapsed. And then my grandfather died, which was a large source of grief for me to deal with. So the uncontrollable, the unpredictable kept arising.

The final motivating factor was a Buddhist talk I listened to that led us to dwell on the certainty of aging and death. This helped me to realise that time was running out: our distant dream of moving to the country had the potential to stay a distant dream for our entire lives, but acknowledging that life is short moved us to finally take action.

I spoke to Camilla on the telephone a couple of months after this interview and after she had moved her family to the country. How was it going? 'I can't believe we didn't do this years ago,' she answered.

This is not to say that all mothers should reduce their hours and move to the country. Other mothers might examine their conditions and find it helps to work more and move to the city. The point is rather that Camilla considered the conditions affecting her daily behaviour and saw that, for her, they were not conducive to freedom from suffering and stress. As a Buddhist, Camilla is engaged in setting up the conditions that bring about awareness and clear-seeing, always chipping away at the ignorance that leads to *dukkha*.

When we learn that so many forces within and outside us condition our actions, many of us start to question whether we have any free will at all or whether all we can do is slavishly follow our conditioning. Yet our reality runs between free choice on the one hand and the powerful force of conditions. With conscious awareness, with clear-seeing, we find opportunities to exercise more free choice rather than follow our conditioning. The Buddha taught that we can intercept our karma, let go of the cravings that cause us to suffer (the Second Noble Truth) and experience, in any moment, the end of suffering (the Third Noble Truth). We just need to set up the conditions that allow clear-seeing to flourish. And we do this by following the Buddha's Eightfold Path (the Fourth Noble Truth).

Of course, we do not always have the power to change our conditions—we cannot change the weather, we may not be able to eject certain difficult characters from our lives. Such circumstances require what Buddhists call 'patience with conditions'. It is slightly amusing, if you have a taste for black humour, to consider the typical Buddhist retreat where one might imagine sits a group of tolerant, kind meditators full of love and goodwill for each other. Yet the average retreatant is a work-in-progress embroiled in an intense experience. The teacher running the retreat hears complaints about: loud breathers in the meditation hall, noisy late-comers, and slow (but very mindful!) movers in the kitchen who hold up everyone in the queue. While some meditators experience bliss and peace in the meditation hall, others struggle to control the effects of the vegetarian diet of chick peas, lentils and cabbage. In all these circumstances it is useful to adopt the mantra 'patience with conditions'.

Practising patience with conditions is a way to become less reactive. We train ourselves to be less explosive, less impulsive, as we cultivate mind states of equanimity where external conditions no longer affect us quite so much. It has become a running joke between Camilla and me: whenever one of us complains about anything, the other adopts a knowing look and a philosophical tone, and slowly re-states the mantra, *patience with conditions*. So if you cannot throw in your stressful job, cannot quite justify leaving your troubled marriage or cannot move to the country, the only alternative, if we want to awaken, is to learn patience with conditions. Change your own mind—never easy, but well worth the effort.

WHAT DOES IT MEAN TO AWAKEN?

I have to confess that I have always struggled in my understanding of the Third Noble Truth, that *suffering can end*. It makes perfect sense to me if I add the words *in any moment*. We can stop the suffering of the moment by letting go of our habitual reactions and choosing more skilful ones—for example, giving up self-centred thinking and fully experiencing the moment. This would definitely be an awakening in that moment. This is how many Buddhists around the world, particularly Zen Buddhists, interpret the idea of awakening. However, I struggle with the other interpretation of awakening, which suggests that suffering can end once and for all, that I could free my mind from the pull of ego and every skerrick of greed, anger and delusion once and for all, as the Buddha seemed to.

Since several Buddhist teachers I have listened to favour this second interpretation, I have worried that I might be the great fraud of the Buddhist community for I lack the faith that this kind of enlightenment might ever happen for me. Therefore it was with some relief that I read the book *After the Ecstasy, the Laundry* by Jack Kornfield. A former monk, Jack Kornfield is one of the senior Buddhist teachers of the Insight tradition, and has reached a conclusion based on his vast experiences, which include meeting numerous Buddhists from all traditions. Here is the opening paragraph:

Enlightenment does exist. It is possible to awaken. Unbounded freedom and joy, oneness with the Divine, awakening into a state of timeless grace—these experiences are more common than you know, and not far away. There is one further truth, however: They don't last. Our realisations and awakenings show us the reality of the world, and they bring transformation, but they pass . . . there is no such thing as enlightened retirement.

His book is full of interviews with those who have experienced spiritual awakenings. His final opinion on the enlightenment question seems to echo that of Zen master Suzuki Roshi, who he quotes: 'Strictly speaking, there are no enlightened people, there is only enlightened activity.'

Since awakening cannot be captured in words, the Buddha used metaphors and images to describe the experience, but from my own investigations of his exact words, it is difficult to tell whether he saw awakening as temporary or permanent. Then again, he definitely taught us that nothing is permanent: could awakening be the only exception?

Maybe I should give the last word on this topic to the French monk described by neuroscientists as 'the happiest man in the world'— Matthieu Ricard, who practises in the Tibetan tradition. To look at his photo, you are inclined to believe he really is the happiest man in the world, although I guess good looks can have that effect. Despite being considered one of the most promising biologists of his generation, Ricard abandoned his scientific career in 1972 to study Buddhism in Darjeeling. This is what he wrote on the final page of his book, *Happiness: A Guide to Developing Life's Most Important Skill*.

The good fortune of meeting with remarkable people who were both wise and compassionate . . . proved to me that one can become enduringly free and happy, providing one knows how to go about it. When I am among friends, I share their lives joyfully.

When I am alone, in my retreat or elsewhere, every passing moment is a delight. When I undertake a project in active life, I rejoice if it is successful; and if it doesn't work out, I see no reason to fret over it, having tried to do my best.

He makes lasting happiness sound so simple, so readily available. To him, it's just a skill. In interviews he often refers to how most people live like beggars, unaware of the treasure buried beneath their shack.

Not only Matthieu but also Vijay, who I mentioned in Chapter 9, appear to be enjoying a lasting experience of awakening. I quoted the words of Jack Kornfield to Vijay when last I saw him and asked, 'Given such an experienced practitioner as Jack Kornfield believes there is no enlightened retirement, do you think it is possible for you to backslide to the way you used to be?' Vijay replied, 'I suppose it is possible, but once you have experienced life without attachment why would you go back to your old ways, which only made you suffer?'

After I emailed this section to him for his comment and to verify his quotation he conceded that the bliss and ecstasy of an enlightenment experience definitely disappeared but the knowledge of another way to be in the world did not:

Maintaining that state is as effortless as Matthieu makes it sound. After knowing the truth it takes as much effort to resist attachment as it takes to stop me from hitting my head against a wall. So I am yet to see a way to unlearn the futility of me and my desires.

I wondered, given Vijay is yet to marry his girlfriend, if having children might eventually threaten his equanimity . . . He thought not.

Yet the most inspiring gem from Vijay is this: 'If my experience was made for special people then I should be the last one to have this experience because I belong to the most common breed on the planet. I'm an Indian software engineer.'

When it comes to enlightenment, I might just practise surrendering to the mystery. I do not know, I do not have the answers, so I will approach the whole area with openness and curiosity, in full acceptance of my not-knowing.

REALISE THE END OF SUFFERING

Although the Third Noble Truth is usually translated as 'Suffering can end', a more complete translations is: 'Suffering can end and this is to be realised'. That is, we need to actively realise, or notice, the times when stress, tension or anxiety have ended, the times when we have successfully let go of craving, be it the craving to act on our anger, to buy something we do not need, or to resist becoming mired in unhelpful thoughts.

And why not notice, deeply observing, when we feel happy? Too often we do not appreciate we were happy until we are unhappy. We do not appreciate we felt healthy until we fall sick. Perhaps we could pay more attention, and practise appreciation and gratitude more often. Savour those feelings of happiness. Resist clinging to them, but consider enjoying them more fully, more mindfully. Be there for them. Show up.

Inquiry

• When you feel down or flat, do you instantly think about shuffling and shifting the externals in your life? Would you consider turning inward instead rather than always relying on the world outside you to make you happy?

- Have you considered trying to enjoy your errands and chores, being present and accepting of your duties rather than stressed and impatient?
- Can you see how being happy for others' good news increases your own happiness and sense of connectedness?
- Do you ever check that your love for others has all the necessary components as taught by the Buddha: lovingkindness, sympathetic joy, compassion and equanimity?
- Have you created the necessary balance in your lifestyle to make a sense of well-being possible?
- If you struggle with your diet, have you explored the deeper issues driving you to food or are you still stuck at the stage of desperately policing what passes your lips?
- Do you regularly question your perceptions, given that most of them are deluded, failing to recognise causes, conditions, processes and impermanence?
- With your current lifestyle, are you setting up the conditions for peace and contentment or the opposite?
- For conditions you cannot change, is there room in your mind to practise 'patience with conditions'?
- Do you ever pause to 'realise' when you have successfully let go of craving?
- Do you pay attention when you are happy, all the more to savour it?

here's an idea . . .

As I mentioned in Chapter 9, the Buddha listed several antidotes for each of the hindrances, but there were two that applied to all Five Hindrances: Noble Friendship and Suitable Conversation. In fact, the Buddha put strong emphasis on the need to belong to a spiritual community, as in this quotation from the scriptures.

> Ananda, Lord Buddha's long-time personal attendant and monk-disciple, asks Buddha: 'Lord, is it true what has been said, that good spiritual friends are fully half of the holy life?'
>
> The Master replied, 'Good friends are the whole of the holy life, not half. The whole.'

Senior Buddhist teacher Subhana often quotes this scripture and has experienced its truth in her own life. Over two decades ago she made a formal commitment to three Buddhist women to provide spiritual friendship to each other. Each woman has moved from the original town where they initially met and they have not managed to stay in regular contact over the years, yet the commitment remains and when they finally do meet each other the connection is still deep.

Inspired by her example, Camilla and I joined Buddhist women Tina and Betsy to make a similar commitment, adopting for ourselves the slightly hippie moniker of 'Dharma Sisters'. Initially we met every six weeks, then stopped meeting as lives became busier and Camilla moved. Tina too will be moving to the country within the year. Yet the commitment remains and our occasional reunions feed us on a deep level. For the time being, three of us still see each other at our weekly Buddhist group and phone or email each other occasionally. It is a great and rare blessing to be able to discuss spiritual matters freely in a small group, sharing all our questions, moral dilemmas and personal problems as well as success stories.

The challenge of living spiritually in the modern world is in hanging in there. The world promises so many delights and distractions that it is easy to neglect the spiritual side of our lives for long periods, or to make it a compartment of our lives with little effect on our day-to-day. To have any hope of living a spiritual life in an ongoing way—a life that acknowledges how much more we can be than our ego dictates—we need spiritual friends. The Buddha knew that personal connections to other practitioners are the most effective way to secure ourselves on the path.

Of course, making spiritual friends if we don't already have some is hardly a swift business that we can put on our 'to do' list and tick off within the week, and it hardly helps that such a large part of any meeting of Buddhists takes place in complete silence. It might take years, as it did for me, to meet the kind of women that Subhana and I have found. Yet I can't help feeling that any strong intention to create such connections will eventually come to fruition and reward us profoundly.

Thich Nhat Hanh's fourteen mindfulness trainings

1. The First Mindfulness Training: Openness

Aware of the suffering created by fanaticism and intolerance, we are determined not to be idolatrous about or bound to any doctrine, theory, or ideology, even Buddhist ones. Buddhist teachings are guiding means to help us learn to look deeply and to develop our understanding and compassion. They are not doctrines to fight, kill, or die for.

2. The Second Mindfulness Training: Nonattachment from Views

Aware of the suffering created by attachment to views and wrong perceptions, we are determined to avoid being narrow-minded and bound to present views. We shall learn and practise nonattachment from views in order to be open to others' insights and experiences. We are aware that the knowledge we presently possess is not changeless, absolute truth. Truth is found in life, and we will observe life within and around us in every moment, ready to learn throughout our lives.

3. The Third Mindfulness Training: Freedom of Thought

Aware of the suffering brought about when we impose our views on others, we are committed not to force others, even our children, by any means whatsoever—such as authority, threat, money, propaganda, or indoctrination—to adopt our views. We will respect the right of others to be different and to choose what to believe and how to decide. We will, however, help others renounce fanaticism and narrowness through practising deeply and engaging in compassionate dialogue.

4. The Fourth Mindfulness Training: Awareness of Suffering

Aware that looking deeply at the nature of suffering can help us develop compassion and find ways out of suffering, we are determined not to avoid or close our eyes before suffering. We are committed to finding ways, including personal contact, images, and sounds, to be with those who suffer, so we can understand their situation deeply and help them transform their suffering into compassion, peace, and joy.

5. The Fifth Mindfulness Training: Simple, Healthy Living

Aware that true happiness is rooted in peace, solidity, freedom, and compassion, and not in wealth or fame, we are determined not to take as the aim of our life fame, profit, wealth, or sensual pleasure, nor to accumulate wealth while millions are hungry and dying. We are committed to living simply and sharing our time, energy, and material resources with those in need. We will practise mindful consuming, not using alcohol, drugs, or any other products that bring toxins into our own and the collective body and consciousness.

6. The Sixth Mindfulness Training: Dealing with Anger

Aware that anger blocks communication and creates suffering, we are determined to take care of the energy of anger when it arises and to recognise and transform the seeds of anger that lie deep in our consciousness. When anger comes up, we are determined not to do or say anything, but to practise mindful breathing or mindful walking and acknowledge, embrace, and look deeply into our anger. We will learn to look with the eyes of compassion at ourselves and at those we think are the cause of our anger.

7. The Seventh Mindfulness Training: Dwelling Happily in the Present Moment

Aware that life is available only in the present moment and that it is possible to live happily in the here and now, we are committed to training ourselves to live deeply each moment of daily life. We will try not to lose ourselves in dispersion or be carried away by regrets about the past, worries about the future, or craving, anger, or jealousy in the present. We will practise mindful breathing to come back to what is happening in the present moment. We are determined to learn the art of mindful living by touching the wondrous, refreshing, and healing elements that are inside and around us, and by nourishing seeds of joy, peace, love, and understanding in ourselves, thus facilitating the work of transformation and healing in our consciousness.

8. The Eighth Mindfulness Training: Community and Communication

Aware that lack of communication always brings separation and suffering, we are committed to training ourselves in the practice of compassionate listening and loving speech. We will learn to listen deeply without judging or reacting and refrain from uttering words that can create discord or cause the community to break. We will make every effort to keep communications open and to reconcile and resolve all conflicts, however small.

9. The Ninth Mindfulness Training: Truthful and Loving Speech
Aware that words can create suffering or happiness, we are committed to learning to speak truthfully and constructively, using only words that inspire hope and confidence. We are determined not to say untruthful things for the sake of personal interest or to impress people, nor to utter words that might cause division or hatred. We will not spread news that we do not know to be certain nor criticise or condemn things of which we are not sure. We will do our best to speak out about situations of injustice, even when doing so may threaten our safety.

10. The Tenth Mindfulness Training: Protecting the Sangha
Aware that the essence and aim of a Sangha is the practice of understanding and compassion, we are determined not to use the Buddhist community for personal gain or profit or transform our community into a political instrument. A spiritual community should, however, take a clear stand against oppression and injustice and should strive to change the situation without engaging in partisan conflicts.

11. The Eleventh Mindfulness Training: Right Livelihood
Aware that great violence and injustice have been done to our environment and society, we are committed not to live with a vocation that is harmful to humans and nature. We will do our best to select a livelihood that helps realise our ideal of understanding and compassion. Aware of global economic, political and social realities, we will behave responsibly as consumers and as citizens, not supporting companies that deprive others of their chance to live.

12. The Twelfth Mindfulness Training: Reverence for Life
Aware that much suffering is caused by war and conflict, we are determined to cultivate nonviolence, understanding, and compassion

in our daily lives, to promote peace education, mindful mediation, and reconciliation within families, communities, nations, and in the world. We are determined not to kill and not to let others kill. We will diligently practise deep looking with our Sangha to discover better ways to protect life and prevent war.

13. The Thirteenth Mindfulness Training: Generosity

Aware of the suffering caused by exploitation, social injustice, stealing, and oppression, we are committed to cultivating lovingkindness and learning ways to work for the well-being of people, animals, plants, and minerals. We will practise generosity by sharing our time, energy, and material resources with those who are in need. We are determined not to steal and not to possess anything that should belong to others. We will respect the property of others, but will try to prevent others from profiting from human suffering or the suffering of other beings.

14. The Fourteenth Mindfulness Training: Right Conduct

Aware that sexual relations motivated by craving cannot dissipate the feeling of loneliness but will create more suffering, frustration, and isolation, we are determined not to engage in sexual relations without mutual understanding, love, and a long-term commitment. In sexual relations, we must be aware of future suffering that may be caused. We know that to preserve the happiness of ourselves and others, we must respect the rights and commitments of ourselves and others. We will do everything in our power to protect children from sexual abuse and to protect couples and families from being broken by sexual misconduct. We will treat our bodies with respect and preserve our vital energies (sexual, breath, spirit) for the realisation of our bodhisattva ideal. We will be fully aware of the responsibility of bringing new lives into the world, and will meditate on the world into which we are bringing new beings.

acknowledgements

DESPITE BEING A RELATIVELY shy and private person, Camilla has generously allowed me to share some of her most personal experiences. She has been kind with her time and her knowledge, and I am so grateful that she still manages to visit Sydney a few times each year. I also acknowledge support and contributions from my Dharma sisters Betsy and Tina.

Senior teacher in the Zen and Insight traditions, Subhana Barzaghi has helped me with all three of my books and is always insightful and supportive. Fiona Clarke from Rigpa has made time to think deeply and review several quotations for this book, and has inspired me with her commitment to the Dharma at each encounter. My mother Sue donated generous hours of her time to help me type interview transcripts.

Thank you to Rachel Springfield in Texas who allowed me to quote from her blog, to Chris Wagner at Lifeline and to former biography client Mendel Factor. I would also like to acknowledge the teachers Stephen Batchelor, Jason Siff, Winton Higgins, Chris MacLean, Patrick Kearney and Christopher Titmuss, whose teachings I draw on for my personal practice.

Other wise friends I have quoted include Vivienne Hartley, Chris Condon and a handful of others who prefer to remain nameless due to the nature of their disclosures.

For permissions I thank those at Thich Nhat Hanh's mindfulnessbell. org website and Parallax Press, his publishers, for the poem 'Call Me By My True Names'.

Thanks to everyone at Allen & Unwin, particularly Annette Barlow, Angela Handley, Catherine Milne and Catherine Taylor for their encouragement and good cheer.

Thank you to all my family members, but especially Zac and Alex, my best teachers and a couple of truly great kids.

bibliography

Ajahn Sundara, 'On Fear & Fearlessness', *Inquiring Mind: A Semiannual Journal of the Vipassana Community*, Spring 2003, p. 5

Batchelor, Stephen, *Buddhism Without Beliefs*, Riverhead Books, a division of G.P. Putnam's Sons, New York, 1997, pp. 5, 97–8

Boorstein, Sylvia, *Don't Just Do Something, Sit There*, HarperCollins, New York, 1996

Boucher, Sandy, *Opening the Lotus: A Woman's Guide to Buddhism*, Beacon Press, Boston, 1997, pp. 112–13

Brett, Samantha, 'Why Women Cheat' <http://blogs.theage.com.au/lifestyle/asksam/archives/2008/07/why-women-cheat.html>

Brooks, Karen, *Consuming Innocence: Popular Culture and Our Children*, University of Queensland Press, Brisbane, 2008, pp. 231, 250–1

Buddha Dharma Education Association, 'Talking to Children about Death', <www.buddhanet.net/r_talkcn.htm>, [24 July 2008]

Burns, Sara, *A Path for Parents: What Buddhism Can Offer*, Windhorse Publications, Birmingham, 2007, pp. 33–4

Buttrose, Ita, and Adams, Penny, *Motherguilt: Australian Women Reveal their True Feelings About Motherhood*, Viking, Camberwell, 2005

Cassidy, Anne, *Parents Who Think Too Much: Why We Do it, How to Stop*, Bantam Doubleday Dell Publishing Group, New York, 1998, pp. 68–9, 95–6, 209–10

Commonwealth of Australia, *Talking with Your Kids about Drugs*, AGPS, Canberra, August 2007

Deveson, Anne, *Resilience*, Allen & Unwin, Sydney, 2003, p. 27

Donahoo, Daniel, *Idolising Children: Why We Should Respect, Not Revere, Our Children*, UNSW Press, Sydney, 2007

Dowrick, Stephanie, *Choosing Happiness: Life and Soul Essentials*, Allen & Unwin, Sydney, 2005, p. 132

——'Calm Children', <www.stephaniedowrick.com/index.php?option=com_content&task=view&id=107&Itemid=29>, [24 July 2008]

——'Welcome, stranger', *Good Weekend* magazine, *The Sydney Morning Herald*, 23 August 2008

——'Happy children, happy parents', <www.stephaniedowrick.com/index.php?option=com_content&task=view&id=114&Itemid=29>, [10 September 2009]

Easwaran, Eknath, (translator), *The Dhammapada*, Nilgiri Press, Tomales, 2007, p. 218

Edelman, Sarah, *Change Your Thinking: Positive and Practical Ways to Overcome Stress, Negative Emotions and Self-Defeating Behaviour Using CBT*, ABC Books, Sydney, 2002, p. 109

Elberse, Anita, 'Should You Invest in the Long Tail?', *Harvard Business Review*, <http://harvardbusinessonline.hbsp.harvard.edu/hbsp/hbr/articles/article.jsp;jsessionid=W2B2JYMAHOPXOAKRGWDR5VQBKE0YIISW?ml_action=get-article&articleID=R0807H&ml_issueid=BR0807&ml_subscriber=true&pageNumber=1&_requestid=361346>, [11 August 2008]

Factor, Mendel, *When War Came*, LhR Press, Sydney, 2005, pp. 154–6

Ferrucci, Piero, *The Gifts of Parenting: Learning and Growing with our Children*, Pan Macmillan Australia, Sydney, 1999, p. 11

Field, Joanna (pen-name of Marion Milner), *A Life of One's Own*, J.P. Tarcher, New York, 1981, pp. 87, 109, 170–1

Freud, Sigmund, 'On Narcissism: An Introduction', 1914

Gandhi, Mohandas Karamchan, 'Truth', *Harijan*, 24 November 1933

Gelin, Martha, Dr, *The Sex Explanation Handbook: Talking with Kids about Sex*, Second edition, Orion South Pty Ltd, Bathurst, 2007, pp. 7–13

Gilbert, Daniel, 'Does Fatherhood Make You Happy?', *Time* magazine, <www.time.com/time/magazine/article/0,9171,1202940-2,00.html>, [8 September 2008]

Gilbert, Elizabeth, *Eat Pray Love: One Woman's Search for Everything*, Bloomsbury, London, 2007, pp. 163–4

Hamilton, Maggie, *What's Happening to Our Girls?*, Viking, Melbourne, 2008, pp. 149, 228

Kabat-Zinn, Jon, *Wherever You Go, There You Are: Mindfulness Meditation in Everyday Life*, Hyperion, New York, 1995

Kabat-Zinn, Myla and Jon, *Everyday Blessings: The Inner Work of Mindful Parenting*, Hyperion, New York, 1997, p. 121

Kirshenbaum, Mira, *When Good People Have Affairs*, St Martin's Press, New York, 2008

Kornfield, Jack, *After the Ecstasy, the Laundry: How the Heart Grows Wise on the Spiritual Path*, Rider Books, London, 2000, pp. xiii, xx

Ladd, Kylie and Langtree, Leigh, *Naked: Confessions of Adultery and Infidelity*, Allen & Unwin, Sydney, 2008

Levine, Madeline, *The Price of Privilege: How Parental Pressure and Material Advantage Are Creating a Generation of Disconnected and Unhappy Kids*, HarperCollins, New York, 2006

Lumby, Catherine and Fine, Duncan, *Why TV is Good for Kids: Raising 21st Century Children*, Pan Macmillan Australia, Sydney, 2006, pp. 71, 254–8

Mackenzie, Vicki, *Why Buddhism? Westerners in Search of Wisdom*, Allen & Unwin, Sydney, 2001, pp. 13–14

Maezen Miller, Karen, *Momma Zen: Walking the Crooked Path of Motherhood*, Trumpeter, Boston, 2006, pp. 100, 106

Nanamoli Thera, *The Life of the Buddha*, Buddhist Publishing Society, Kandy, 1992, pp. 175–6

Noonan, Gerard, 'Lesson for the school of hard Knox', *The Sydney Morning Herald*, 24 November 2007

Quart, Alissa, *Hothouse Kids: The Dilemma of the Gifted Child*, Penguin Press, New York, 2006

Ricard, Matthieu, *Happiness: A Guide to Developing Life's Most Important Skill*, Atlantic Books, London, 2007, p. 266

Rossmanith, Angela, *When Will the Children Play: Finding Time for Childhood*, Mandarin, Sydney, 1997

Salzberg, Sharon, *Faith: Trusting Your Own Deepest Experience*, Riverhead Hardcover, New York, 2002

Seligman, Martin, *The Optimistic Child: A Revolutionary Approach to Raising Resilient Children*, Random House Australia, Sydney, 1995, pp. 27, 44

Solzhenitsyn, Aleksandr, *The Gulag Archipelago: 1918–1956: An Experiment in Literary Investigation*, Volume II, Harper & Row, New York, 1975, pp. 615–17

Springfield, Rachel, *Mama's So Mindful . . . or tryin' to be!*, <mamasomindful.blogspot.com>, 2 June 2008, 20 June 2008, 29 May 2008

Stoppard, Miriam, *Questions Children Ask and How to Answer Them*, Dorling Kindersley, London, 1997, pp. 46–7

Sullivan, Jane, 'Let's talk about sex, ladies', *The Sydney Morning Herald*, 5 July 2008

Titmuss, Christopher, *Light on Enlightenment: Revolutionary Teachings on the Inner Life*, Shambhala, Boston, 1999, pp. 117–20

Tolle, Eckhart, *A New Earth: Awakening to Your Life's Purpose*, Penguin Group (Australia), Melbourne, 2005, pp. 298–9

Thich Nhat Hanh, *Being Peace*, Parallax Press, Berkeley, 1987, p. 79

——*Living Buddha, Living Christ*, Riverhead Books, New York, 1995, pp. 2, 5–6

——*The Fourteen Mindfulness Trainings Introduction*, <www.mindfulnessbell.org/14trainings.htm>, [15 September 2008]

UNICEF, *The State of the World's Children 2006*, <www.unicef.org/sowc06/press/who.php>, [11 August 2008]

——*The State of the World's Children 2008*, <www.unicef.org/sowc08/docs/sowc08.pdf>, [11 August 2008]

index